GUARDIANS' BONDS

OF

ALBEMARLE COUNTY, VIRGINIA

1783 - 1852

. . . .

Compiled and Published

By

Mary Catharine Murphy

Instructor in Genealogical Research

University of Virginia School of General Studies

1968

Copyright 1968
By: Mary Catherine Murphy

Copyright Transferred 1984
To: Southern Historical Press, Inc.

All rights reserved. No part of this publication may be reproduced, stored in a retrieval system, transmitted in any form, posted on to the web in any form or by any means without the prior written permission of the publisher.

Please direct all correspondence and orders to:

www.southernhistoricalpress.com
or
SOUTHERN HISTORICAL PRESS, Inc.
PO BOX 1267
375 West Broad Street
Greenville, SC   29601
southernhistoricalpress@gmail.com

ISBN #0-89308-939-7

Printed in the United States of America

TO THE MEMORY OF

MY MOTHER

NANNIE ELIZABETH (GEORGE) PAYNE

1881 - 1965

CONTENTS

PREFACE

SECTION I
    LOOSE BONDS 1783-1824   LB,1

SECTION II
    BOND BOOK 1829-1844   II,1

SECTION III
    BOND BOOK 1844-1852   III,1

INDEX   INDEX,1

ILLUSTRATIONS

GUARDIAN'S BOND (handwritten) FOR MERIWETHER LEWIS,
    1786   viii

PORTION OF HANDWRITTEN JOURNAL OF IRA GARRETT,
    ALBEMARLE COUNTY CLERK   9,10

GUARDIAN'S BOND (printed) FOR JULIA A. BROCKMAN   xii

Know all men by these Presents, that we William Meriwether and Nicholas Lewis Gent. are held and firmly bound unto James Minor, James Kerr, Bennett Henderson and John Key Gent. in the sum of three thousand pounds to the payment of which we bind ourselves our Heirs our joint & separate Heirs &c firmly by these presents Given under our hands & seals this 14th of Sepr. 1786

Whereas William Meriwether is appointed a Guardian to Meriwether Lewis an Orphan Infant son to Wm. Lewis decd. The condition of this Obligation is such that if the said William Meriwether do well and truly perform the part of a Guardian by attending to the education of the said Orphan, rendering a true acct. & of the whole of sd. Orphans Estate when called on, and acting in every respect as Guardian to sd. Orphan then this Obligation to be void otherwise to remain in full force & effect —

Wm. Meriwether (Seal)

Nicholas Lewis (Seal)

PREFACE

It is the purpose of this volume to make available to researchers the quantity of very specific information contained in the existing GUARDIANS' BONDS of Albemarle County, Virginia, covering the years 1783 through 1852. For some unknown reason this material escaped detection by the microfilmers, and apparently has been unknown until this presentation.

These guardians' bonds exist in two forms. Those comprising the earliest group, 1783 through 1824, are loose and scattered in and among other old papers. Abstracts of this group are presented herewith in chronological order in Section I. In my index, the names appearing in this group are designated by "LB" (for "Loose Bonds") followed by the page of Section I on which the name appears.

The bonds for the later periods were carefully pasted into two books many years ago, probably by Albemarle County Clerk Ira Garrett. These bonds are given here in the order in which they appear in those books, and this is, generally speaking, chronologically. The first of the two pasted bond books covers the years 1829 through 1844, and is presented herewith as Section II, and names in it are designated in my index as "II" followed by the appropriate page number. My pagination for this Section II (as well as Section III) follows exactly the pagination of the Bond Books themselves. Therefore the page number given in my index for this volume is also the exact page on which that name appears in the Albemarle County Bond Book. This system was used in order to provide an index for the Albemarle County Bond Books simultaneously. Not only had these Bond Books been unknown; they are also unindexed.

Treatment of Bond Book 1844 through 1852 in Section III follows exactly the same format as set forth above: my index using the designation "III" followed by the appropriate page number.

It will be noted that in these two Bond Books there appears a bond only about every other page. When these bonds were pasted into the books, apparently it was decided to use this system which allowed for an occasional note to be pasted on a facing page. These notes usually were requests by orphans for a particular guardian, and in some instances stated the age of the orphan, or the relationship of the requested guardian to the orphan. Whenever such information appeared, note of it was appended to my abstract of the corresponding bond. As can be deduced from examining my abstracts, about 90% of the facing pages in these Bond Books were blank.

Further, it should be brought to the researcher's attention that in abstracting this material, every effort was made to include all pertinent information. The early bonds were handwritten and the later ones were executed on a printed form which varied slightly from time to time. The information given was essentially the same, however.

In the abstracts, it may be assumed that the name given as "Parent" is that of the DECEASED parent. In a few instances the word "deceased" had been scratched through very definitely in the printed forms, and these instances are remarked in my abstracts by the words "not deceased" in brackets under the name of the parent IF he were not the individual being appointed guardian. Where the father was not deceased and was himself being appointed guardian to his own children, I have so indicated by the word "father" in brackets immediately preceding his name in the guardian category.

In some cases the name of the parent (presumably deceased) and the name of the guardian were identical. It would be exceedingly unwise to leap to the conclusion that they were necessarily one and the same person and that the Clerk may have failed to delete the word "deceased"; often they were brothers, uncles, grandfathers, etc., bearing the same name. If any information came to light concerning this relationship, I have included it in brackets.

As always, the spelling of all names was at the discretion and whim of whatever Clerk or Deputy wrote the bond, and frequently this spelling varied within the same document. Whenever the individual's signature was legible, it seemed appropo to accept his spelling of his own name over that of the Clerk's choosing. Unfortunately, the orphan and his deceased parent had no opportunity to sign the bond, so the most important spelling of their names frequently remains a mystery. In the index an effort was made to equate the factors involved therein by cross-indexing as many varieties of the surnames as possible.

The handwritten journal, a portion of which is reproduced on pages 9 and 10, and an explanation of which appears on page 8, is presumably that of Clerk Ira Garrett. It was useful only for this period of missing bonds from 1792 through 1797. I did find some bonds for those years and present them herewith in chronological order, but those particular bonds were NOT listed by Mr. Garrett, and I was unable to locate those he DID list for that period. Incidentally, his continuing list also did not cover the bonds I was able to find and include herewith for the years 1798 through 1805. Mr. Garrett had no other bonds on his list which I did not find in the original.

According to the Rev. Edgar Woods' Albemarle County in Virginia, the Albemarle County Clerks during the period covered by these existing bonds, were: John Nicholas (1750-1792), his son John Nicholas (1792-1815), Alexander Garrett (1815-1831), and his brother Ira Garrett (1831-post Civil War). Most of these men served as Deputy Clerks before their appointments as Clerks, and Ira Garrett was again a Deputy Clerk after the military appointment of his successor as Clerk.

For completion of this volume I am indebted to many individuals who would probably prefer to remain anonymous. However these cannot escape acknowledgment: Mrs. Eva White Maupin, retired Clerk of the Albemarle County and Circuit Courts, without whose interest and help I could never have attempted this project; her successor in office, Mrs. Shelby Marshall, who kindly allowed me continued access to the material; Mr. J. Fred Dorman and Mr. George H. S. King who graciously gave advice on the format; and last but not least, my husband, Teddy, and daughters, Diana and Belinda, who cheerfully managed to survive the ordeal.

Mary Catharine Murphy
(Mrs. Theodore Murphy)

1837 Fendall Avenue
Charlottesville, Virginia 22903

KNOW all men by these presents, that we Wiley Dickenson & Ambrose Brockman are held and firmly bound unto John Watson, James Old, Parmenius Rogers & John Rodes Gent'emen, Justices of the Court of Albemarle county, now sitting, in the sum of One thousand Dollars to the payment whereof well and truly to be made to the said Justices, and their successors, we bind ourselves, and each of us, and each of our heirs, executors, and administrators jointly and severally, firmly by these presents. Sealed with our seals and dated this 2nd day of May Anno Dom. one thousand eight hundred Eight and in the 32d year of the Commonwealth.

THE condition of the above obligation is such, that if the above bound Wiley Dickenson executors and administrators, shall well and truly pay and deliver, or cause to be paid and delivered, unto _____ Brockman orphan of Samuel Brockman deceased, all such estate or estates as now is, or are, or hereafter shall appear to be due to the said orphan when, and as soon as she shall attain to lawful age, or when thereto required by the justices of the said county court, as also keep harmless the above named justices, their and every of their heirs, executors, and administrators, from all trouble and damages that shall or may arise about the said estate; then the above obligation to be void, otherwise to remain in full force.

Sealed and delivered in the presence of

Alex Garrett

Wiley Dickenson
A Brockman

SECTION I

LOOSE BONDS

1783 - 1824

LOOSE BONDS, page 1

ORPHAN: William Thompson
PARENT: David Thompson GUARDIAN: John Mullins
DATE: 9 May 1783 AMOUNT OF BOND: 50 pounds
SECURITY: James Harris

. . . .

ORPHAN: Hugh, & Elizabeth Dollins
PARENT: William Dollins GUARDIAN: Hugh Alexander
DATE: 12 June 1783 AMOUNT OF BOND: 200 pounds
SECURITY: John Marks

. . . .

ORPHAN: Eli, & David Melton
PARENT: William Melton GUARDIAN: John Melton
DATE: 11 Oct. 1783 AMOUNT OF BOND: 600 pounds
SECURITY: John Coles

. . . .

ORPHAN: Mary Melton
PARENT: William Melton GUARDIAN: John Melton, Jr.
DATE: 11 Oct. 1783 AMOUNT OF BOND: 300 pounds
SECURITY: John Coles

. . . .

ORPHAN: Austin, & Mary Smith
PARENT: [not given] GUARDIAN: William Flynt
DATE: 9 Dec. 1784 AMOUNT OF BOND: 500 pounds
SECURITY: Frederick William Wills
Note: Bond does not give Austin and Mary Smith's parent's name; it speaks of these children as "legatees of Richard Durrett deceased."

LOOSE BONDS, page 2

ORPHAN: Nelson, Barttelott, & Nancy Meeks
PARENT: Martin Meeks   GUARDIAN: Jonathan Black
DATE: 15 April 1785   AMOUNT OF BOND: 200 pounds
SECURITY: John Denton
          Charles Woodall

. . . .

ORPHAN: Meriwether Lewis
PARENT: William Lewis   GUARDIAN: William Meriwether
DATE: 14 Sept. 1786   AMOUNT OF BOND: 3,000 pounds
SECURITY: Nicholas Lewis

. . . .

ORPHAN: Jane Lewis
PARENT: Charles Lewis   GUARDIAN: Howell Lewis
DATE: 14 Dec. 1786   AMOUNT OF BOND: 1,000 pounds
SECURITY: Isham Lewis

. . . .

ORPHAN: Mary Randolph Lewis
PARENT: Charles Lewis   GUARDIAN: Charles Wingfield, Jr.
DATE: 14 Dec. 1786   AMOUNT OF BOND: 1,000 pounds
SECURITY: Menan Mills

. . . .

ORPHAN: Susan Lewis
PARENT: Charles Lewis   GUARDIAN: Edward Moore
DATE: 18 Dec. 1786   AMOUNT OF BOND: 100 pounds
SECURITY: John Jouett

LOOSE BONDS, page 3

ORPHAN: Susanna Lewis
PARENT: Charles Lewis GUARDIAN: John Carr
DATE: 13 Dec. 1787 AMOUNT OF BOND: 600 pounds
SECURITY: J. Breckinridge

. . . .

ORPHAN: Jechonias Yancey
PARENT: Jere^h Yancey GUARDIAN: James Brooks
DATE: 13 Dec. 1787 AMOUNT OF BOND: 300 pounds
SECURITY: Charles Yancey

. . . .

ORPHAN: Robert, William, & Nancy Clark
PARENT: Micajah Clark GUARDIAN: Jacob Oglesby
DATE: 14 Feb. 1788 AMOUNT OF BOND: 1,500 pounds
SECURITY: Edward Moore

. . . .

ORPHAN: Joel Yancey
PARENT: Jeremiah Yancey GUARDIAN: Margaret Yancey
DATE: 14 Feb. 1788 AMOUNT OF BOND: 300 pounds
SECURITY: Charles Yancey
          James Brooks

. . . .

ORPHAN: Sarah Watson
PARENT: William Watson GUARDIAN: William Gillum
DATE: 10 July 1788 AMOUNT OF BOND: 500 pounds
SECURITY: John Gillum
          Micajah Carr

LOOSE BONDS, page 4

ORPHAN: John Terrill

PARENT: Reubin Terrill GUARDIAN: John Wood

DATE: 11 Dec. 1788 AMOUNT OF BOND: 1,000 pounds

SECURITY: William Grayson

. . . .

ORPHAN: Sally Greening

PARENT: Robert Greening GUARDIAN: Samuel Munday

DATE: [none given] 1789 AMOUNT OF BOND: 200 pounds

SECURITY: Ambrose Dowell

. . . .

ORPHAN: Robert, George, Reuben, William, Matthew, Kesiah, Mary, & Judith Turner

PARENT: Charles Turner GUARDIAN: Maryan Turner

DATE: 10 Sept. 1789 AMOUNT OF BOND: 750 pounds

SECURITY: Robert Turner
James Jones, Sr.

. . . .

ORPHAN: Mildred Watson

PARENT: [none given] GUARDIAN: John Key

DATE: 10 Sept. 1789 AMOUNT OF BOND: 500 pounds

SECURITY: Joshua Key

Note: Bond specifies the guardianship is to guarantee Mildred's receipt of "all the Estate left her by Wm Watson deceased."

. . . .

ORPHAN: Lucy Watson

PARENT: [none given] GUARDIAN: Joshua Key

DATE: 10 Sept. 1789 AMOUNT OF BOND: 500 pounds

SECURITY: John Key

Note: Bond specifies there is "to be paid and Delivered unto Lucy Watson all the estate of Wm Watson deceased."

LOOSE BONDS, page 5

ORPHAN: David, & John Thomson
PARENT: David Thomson   GUARDIAN: Robert Thomson
DATE: 14 Oct. 1789   AMOUNT OF BOND: 500 pounds
SECURITY: John Mullins

. . . .

ORPHAN: Charles Warner Lewis
PARENT: Charles Lewis   GUARDIAN: Howell Lewis
DATE: 11 June 1790   AMOUNT OF BOND: 2,000 pounds
SECURITY: Charles Wingfield, Jr.

. . . .

ORPHAN: Sally Davis
Grand-
PARENT: Lewis Davis   GUARDIAN: Richard Snow
DATE: 14 April 1791   AMOUNT OF BOND: 150 pounds
SECURITY: Lewis Davis, Jr.

. . . .

ORPHAN: Jane Lewis
PARENT: William Lewis   GUARDIAN: Edmund Anderson
DATE: 12 May [no year]   AMOUNT OF BOND: 1,500 pounds
SECURITY: Menan Mills
Note: This bond bore no date, but the group of bonds in which it
was found were dated 1783 through 1791.
. . . .

ORPHAN: Hudson Garland
PARENT: James Garland, Jr.   GUARDIAN: Charles Wingfield
DATE: 14 July 1791   AMOUNT OF BOND: 800 pounds
SECURITY: Walter Leake

LOOSE BONDS, page 6

ORPHAN: Samuel Woodson
PARENT: Tucker Woodson GUARDIAN: Edward Moore
DATE: 9 Sept. 1791 AMOUNT OF BOND: 100 pounds
SECURITY: George Bruce

. . . .

ORPHAN: Walter Key
PARENT: Martin Key GUARDIAN: John Nicholas
DATE: 13 Oct. 1791 AMOUNT OF BOND: 1,500 pounds
SECURITY: John Key

. . . .

ORPHAN: Fanny Bailey
PARENT: Callum Bailey GUARDIAN: Pleasant Oglesby
DATE: 8 Dec. 1791 AMOUNT OF BOND: 500 pounds
SECURITY: Jacob Oglesby

. . . .

ORPHAN: Susannah Henderson
PARENT: John Henderson GUARDIAN: John Clark, Jr.
DATE: 12 Nov. 1791 AMOUNT OF BOND: 1,000 pounds
SECURITY: Menan Mills
          Robert Jouett

. . . .

ORPHAN: Polly Barker
PARENT: [none given] GUARDIAN: John Sneed
DATE: 9 Feb. 1792 AMOUNT OF BOND: 50 pounds
SECURITY: Elijah Sneed

LOOSE BONDS, page 7

ORPHAN: John Cleaveland
PARENT: Reubin Cleaveland   GUARDIAN: Jeremiah Cleveland
DATE: 9 Feb. 1792   AMOUNT OF BOND: 100 pounds
SECURITY: David Gillaspy

. . . .

ORPHAN: Thomas, & William Crosthwait
PARENT: William Crosthwait   GUARDIAN: George Divers
DATE: 13 Dec. 1792   AMOUNT OF BOND: 400 pounds
SECURITY: William Shelton

. . . .

ORPHAN: Mildred Blackwell
PARENT: [none given]   GUARDIAN: Joseph Mills
DATE: 5 Oct. 1795   AMOUNT OF BOND: $4,000
SECURITY: Mathew Rodes

. . . .

ORPHAN: Jane[?] Beck
PARENT: Andrew Beck   GUARDIAN: Cornelius Breedlove
DATE: 7 Dec. 1795   AMOUNT OF BOND: $300
SECURITY: Joseph Beck

. . . .

ORPHAN: Nancy Marks
PARENT: Peter Marks   GUARDIAN: Robert Jouett
DATE: 7 Dec. 1795   AMOUNT OF BOND: $1,500
SECURITY: John Carr

LOOSE BONDS, page 8

ORPHAN: Elizabeth, Mary C., & Martha Marks

PARENT: Peter Marks   GUARDIAN: George Divers

DATE: 4 Jan. 1796   AMOUNT OF BOND: $6,000

SECURITY: Francis Walker

. . . .

ORPHAN: Sophia Marks

PARENT: [none given]   GUARDIAN: George Divers

DATE: 4 Jan. 1796   AMOUNT OF BOND: $3,000

SECURITY: Francis Walker

. . . .

    It was not possible to locate the actual bonds for the 36 entries immediately following, covering the years 1792 through 1797. The only information available on these particular items is contained in what is presumed to be the handwritten journal of the Albemarle County Clerk, Ira Garrett. This journal, pertinent portions of which are reproduced herewith on pages 9 and 10, begins with these 36 items and continues recapping all guardian's bonds through 1852. Since it includes less rather than more information than the bonds themselves, I have used it only in this instance where these 36 actual bonds were not available for reference.

    The idiosyncrasies of Mr. Garrett's handwriting will be apparent; for example his omission of the "s" in the name "Crosthwait" in the very first entry, and his failure to cross the letter "t", not to mention his penchant for writing his capital letters in one fashion and then a moment later writing the same letter in an entirely different way (see "A" as in "Allen", and "B" as in "Berry"). The problem of accurately deciphering Mr. Garrett's writing on the many bonds he handled both as Deputy Clerk and Clerk was a constant one.

LOOSE BONDS, page 9

Guardians appointed by the County Court of Albemarle

Date of Appointment	Names of Wards	Names of Guardians	Names of Securities
1797 Apl. 4	Perry & Ann Owen Cothwait	Shelton Cothwait	George Divers
1794 Oct. 9	Wm Henderson, Sally Henderson, James Henderson, Charles Henderson, Isham Henderson, William Henderson, Elizabeth Henderson, Francis Henderson, Lucy Henderson, Nancy Henderson	John Henderson	Edward Moore
1797 Sep. 4	Richard Sims	James Sims	Ambrose Checkman
1796 Oct. 6	Amy N Carter	Wilson C Nicholas	Jno. Nicholas
1793 June 13	Nancy Lewis	Charles Wingfield Sr.	Thomas Carr
1793 July 11	Wm Watson	Charles Rothwell	Jno Watson
1792 Jan. 14	James Robinson & Wm Robinson	Ralph Barlow	James Gell
1793 July 11	Matthew Watson	John Watson	Charles Rothwell
1793 Sep. 12	Milcard Watson	Jno Watson	Phill Buckner & C. Rothwell
1793 Sep. 12	Jno D Solomon, Mary Solomon	David Clarkson	Peter Clarkson
1793 Sep. 13	John Thompson	Isaiah Gentry	William Woods, Daniel Maupin
1793 Apl. 12	Thomas Solomon, Elizabeth Solomon, Peggy Solomon	David Clarkson	Peter Clarkson
1793 July 11	Mary Hart	Andrew Hart	Walter Leake
1793 July 11	Mary Hart, Samuel D Hart, Elizabeth Hart	Andrew Hart	Walter Leake
1795 Oct.	Catherine Allen	Richard N Allen	William Clarke
1795 Sep.	Dorothea Allen	Richd N Allen	Wm Clarke
1795 Sep. 7	Polly Allen	Richd N Allen	William Clarke
1794 Dec. 11	Rebecca Perry	George Burger	George Berry
1794 Jany 9	Whitticar Carter	Edward Carter	Charles Carter
1794 Jany 9	Will Carter	Edward Carter	Charles Carter
1794 July 10	Martha Edwards	William Ball	Ambrose Edwards
1795 Apl. 7	Patsy M Lee, George M Lee	James Kinsolving	Miriam Miles

LOOSE BONDS, page 10

Date of Appointment			Names of Wards	Names of Guardians	Names of Securities
1794	Nov	13	Tho Boots	Mr Walker	Chiles Terrill
1794	Sept	11	Sarah Linton	Mr Clayton	Andrew Flannagan
1797	Oct	3	Nancy Minor James Minor John Minor	Dabney Minor	George Carr Cornelius Schink William Dalton
1797	Mar	6	Sarah Gillum Nancy Gillum	Thomas Travallors	George Thurmond
1796	Apl	6	Mary C Carter	Wilson C Nicholas	Mr Nicholas
1797	Apl	3	Elizabeth Colvard	James George	John Sleg
1795	July	6	William Wood	James Lewis	Josh Sleg George Bruce
1794	July	10	Milly Flores	Horsley Goodman	David Clarkson
1792	Sept	13	Francis M Washington Ann C Washington	John Tinsley	Charles Tinill James Minor Wm E Merriwether
1792	Sept	13	James Walker	Wm Leigh	Nash Harlow
1795	Mar	5	Sarah Minor	Garland Carr	John Carr
1793	June	17	Sarah Lewis	Joseph Wingfield	Charles Wingfield Thomas Carr
1792	Dec	13	Sally Hopkins	Nich Johnson	Charles Lewis
1797	June	3	Nelson Barkesdale	Saml Barkesdale	Christopher Wingfield

LOOSE BONDS, page 11

ORPHAN: Perry, & Ann Bowen Cro[s]thwait
PARENT: GUARDIAN: Shelton Cro[s]thwait
DATE: 4 Apr. 1797   AMOUNT OF BOND:
SECURITY: George Divers

. . . .

ORPHAN: William, Sally, James, Charles, Isham, Hillsmon, Elizabeth, Francis, Lucy, & Nancy Henderson
PARENT: GUARDIAN: John Henderson
DATE: 9 Oct. 1794   AMOUNT OF BOND:
SECURITY: Edward Moore

. . . .

ORPHAN: Richard Sims
PARENT: GUARDIAN: James Sims
DATE: 4 Sept. 1797   AMOUNT OF BOND:
SECURITY: Ambrose Brockman

. . . .

ORPHAN: Ann W. Carter
PARENT: GUARDIAN: Wilson C. Nicholas
DATE: 6 Apr. 1796   AMOUNT OF BOND:
SECURITY: John Nicholas

. . . .

ORPHAN: Nancy Lewis
PARENT: GUARDIAN: Charles Wingfield, Jr.
DATE: 13 June 1793   AMOUNT OF BOND:
SECURITY: Thomas Carr

LOOSE BONDS, page 12

ORPHAN: William Watson
PARENT: GUARDIAN: Charles Rothwell
DATE: 11 July 1793   AMOUNT OF BOND:
SECURITY: John Watson

. . . .

ORPHAN: James, & William Robinson
PARENT: GUARDIAN: Nathaniel Harlow
DATE: 14 June 1792   AMOUNT OF BOND:
SECURITY: James Bell

. . . .

ORPHAN: Matthew Watson
PARENT: GUARDIAN: John Watson
DATE: 11 July 1793   AMOUNT OF BOND:
SECURITY: Charles Rothwell

. . . .

ORPHAN: Mildred Watson
PARENT: GUARDIAN: John Watson
DATE: 12 Sept. 1793   AMOUNT OF BOND:
SECURITY: Phill Buckner
          Charles Rothwell

. . . .

ORPHAN: John D., & Mary Soloman
PARENT: GUARDIAN: David Clarkson
DATE: 12 Sept. 1793   AMOUNT OF BOND:
SECURITY: Peter Clarkson

LOOSE BONDS, page 13

ORPHAN: John Thompson
PARENT: GUARDIAN: Josiah Gentry
DATE: 13 Sept. 1793   AMOUNT OF BOND:
SECURITY: William Woods
          Daniel Maupin

. . . .

ORPHAN: Thomas, Elizabeth, & Peggy Soloman
PARENT: GUARDIAN: David Clarkson
DATE: 12 Sept. 1793   AMOUNT OF BOND:
SECURITY: Peter Clarkson

. . . .

ORPHAN: Mary Leake
PARENT: GUARDIAN: Andrew Hart
DATE: 11 July 1793   AMOUNT OF BOND:
SECURITY: Walter Leake

. . . .

ORPHAN: Mary, Samuel L., & Elizabeth Hart
PARENT: GUARDIAN: Andrew Hart
DATE: 11 July 1793   AMOUNT OF BOND:
SECURITY: Walter Leake

. . . .

ORPHAN: Catherine Allen
PARENT: GUARDIAN: Richard H. Allen
DATE: Apr. 1795   AMOUNT OF BOND:
SECURITY: William Clarke

LOOSE BONDS, page 14

ORPHAN: Dorotha Allen
PARENT: GUARDIAN: Richard H. Allen
DATE: Apr. 1795   AMOUNT OF BOND:
SECURITY: William Clarke

. . . .

ORPHAN: Polly Allen
PARENT: GUARDIAN: Richard H. Allen
DATE: 7 Apr. 1795   AMOUNT OF BOND:
SECURITY: William Clarke

. . . .

ORPHAN: Rebbecca Berry
PARENT: GUARDIAN: George Burger
DATE: 11 Dec. 1794   AMOUNT OF BOND:
SECURITY: George Berry

. . . .

ORPHAN: Whittico Carter
PARENT: GUARDIAN: Edward Carter
DATE: 9 Jan. 1794   AMOUNT OF BOND:
SECURITY: Charles Carter

. . . .

ORPHAN: Hill Carter
PARENT: GUARDIAN: Edward Carter
DATE: 9 Jan. 1794   AMOUNT OF BOND:
SECURITY: Charles Carter

LOOSE BONDS, page 15

ORPHAN: Martha Edwards
PARENT: GUARDIAN: William Hall
DATE: 10 July 1794   AMOUNT OF BOND:
SECURITY: Ambrose Edwards

. . . .

ORPHAN: Patsey M., & George W. Lee
PARENT: GUARDIAN: James Kinsolving
DATE: 7 Apr. 1795   AMOUNT OF BOND:
SECURITY: Menan Mills

. . . .

ORPHAN: Thomas Boots
PARENT: GUARDIAN: John Walker
DATE: 13 Nov. 1794   AMOUNT OF BOND:
SECURITY: Chiles Terrill

. . . .

ORPHAN: Sarah Linton
PARENT: GUARDIAN: John Clayton
DATE: 11 Sept. 1794   AMOUNT OF BOND:
SECURITY: Ambrose Flannagan

. . . .

ORPHAN: Nancy, James, & John Minor
PARENT: GUARDIAN: Dabney Minor
DATE: 3 Oct. 1797   AMOUNT OF BOND:
SECURITY: George Carr,
Cornelius Schink, William Dalton

LOOSE BONDS, page 16

ORPHAN: Sarah, & Nancy Gillum

PARENT: GUARDIAN: Thomas Travillion

DATE: 6 Mar. 1797   AMOUNT OF BOND:

SECURITY: Benj^{a}[?] Thurmond

. . . .

ORPHAN: Mary C. Carter

PARENT: GUARDIAN: Wilson C. Nicholas

DATE: 8 Apr. 1794   AMOUNT OF BOND:

SECURITY: John Nicholas

. . . .

ORPHAN: Elizabeth Colvard

PARENT: GUARDIAN: James George

DATE: 3 Apr. 1797   AMOUNT OF BOND:

SECURITY: John Key

. . . .

ORPHAN: William Wood

PARENT: GUARDIAN: James Lewis

DATE: 6 July 1795   AMOUNT OF BOND:

SECURITY: Joshua Key
              George Bruce

. . . .

ORPHAN: Milly Rodes

PARENT: GUARDIAN: Horsley Goodman

DATE: 10 July 1794   AMOUNT OF BOND:

SECURITY: David Clarkson

LOOSE BONDS, page 17

ORPHAN: Francis M., & Ann C. Washington

PARENT: GUARDIAN: John Tinsley

DATE: 13 Sept. 1792   AMOUNT OF BOND:

SECURITY: Charles Terrill,
Edward Moore, Wm. D. Meriwether

. . . .

ORPHAN: James Walker

PARENT: GUARDIAN: William Leigh

DATE: 13 Sept. 1792   AMOUNT OF BOND:

SECURITY: Nathaniel Harlow

. . . .

ORPHAN: Sarah Minor

PARENT: GUARDIAN: Garland Carr

DATE: 5 Mar. 1795   AMOUNT OF BOND:

SECURITY: John Carr

. . . .

ORPHAN: Sarah E. Lewis

PARENT: GUARDIAN: Joseph Wingfield

DATE: 17 June 1793   AMOUNT OF BOND:

SECURITY: Charles Wingfield
          Thomas Carr

. . . .

ORPHAN: Sally Hopkins

PARENT: GUARDIAN: Richard Johnson

DATE: 13 Dec. 1792   AMOUNT OF BOND:

SECURITY: Charles Lewis

LOOSE BONDS, page 18

ORPHAN: Nelson Barkesdale
PARENT: GUARDIAN: Samuel Barkesdale
DATE: 3 June 1797   AMOUNT OF BOND:
SECURITY: Christopher Wingfield

. . . .

END OF BONDS COPIED FROM Ira Garrett's JOURNAL

* * * * * * * * * * * * *

Resumption of Abstracts from Original Bonds

. . . .

ORPHAN: Richard, & George Matthews Woods
PARENT: Richard Woods   GUARDIAN: James Woods
DATE: 7 Sept. 1801   AMOUNT OF BOND: $10,000
SECURITY: William Woods
          James Brooks

. . . .

ORPHAN: Rush Blain
PARENT: [none given]   GUARDIAN: Edward Fitzpatrick
DATE: 8 Sept. 1801   AMOUNT OF BOND: $100
SECURITY: Walter Leake

. . . .

ORPHAN: William Holmes
PARENT: William Holmes   GUARDIAN: William W. Hening
DATE: 2 Feb. 1802   AMOUNT OF BOND: $50
SECURITY: Robert Phillips

LOOSE BONDS, page 19

ORPHAN: Sally Jefferson Bell

PARENT: Thomas Bell   GUARDIAN: Jesse Scott

DATE: 4 Oct. 1802   AMOUNT OF BOND: $600

SECURITY: Thomas Carr, Jr.
          Peter Lott

. . . .

ORPHAN: John Thacker

PARENT: [none given]   GUARDIAN: James Brooks

DATE: 5 Oct. 1802   AMOUNT OF BOND: $150

SECURITY: William Woods

. . . .

ORPHAN: Nancy Dowell

PARENT: John Dowell   GUARDIAN: Major Dowell
                                            ("son of Thomas")
DATE: 6 Dec. 1802   AMOUNT OF BOND: $2,000

SECURITY: Ambrose Dowell
          James Dowell

. . . .

ORPHAN: Daniel Scott

PARENT: John Scott   GUARDIAN: Samuel Dyer

DATE: 6 Dec. 1802   AMOUNT OF BOND: $6,000

SECURITY: John Harris
          Charles A. Scott

. . . .

ORPHAN: James Gilmer

PARENT: George Gilmer   GUARDIAN: William D. Meriwether

DATE: 2 Jan. 1803   AMOUNT OF BOND: 5,000 pounds

SECURITY: Isaac Miller

LOOSE BONDS, page 20

ORPHAN: Ann Bibbins

PARENT: John Bibbins GUARDIAN: William Alexander

DATE: 3 Jan. 1803 AMOUNT OF BOND: $150

SECURITY: Joshua Catling

. . . .

ORPHAN: James, & Micajah Clark

PARENT: William Clark GUARDIAN: Jacob Clark

DATE: 3 Jan. 1803 AMOUNT OF BOND: $2,000

SECURITY: Matthew Rodes,
David Anderson, John Sandidge, Claiborn Rothwell,
William Clark, Joshua Key, John Rogers

. . . .

ORPHAN: Frances, & Susanna Phillips

PARENT: Stephen Phillips GUARDIAN: Christian Wertenbaker

DATE: 5 April 1803 AMOUNT OF BOND: $500

SECURITY: Matthew Henderson

. . . .

ORPHAN: Susanna, Christian, & Williamson Foster

PARENT: James Foster GUARDIAN: Augustine Shepherd

DATE: 6 June 1803 AMOUNT OF BOND: $1,500

SECURITY: John Clarkson,
Thomas Pettit, James Brooks,
Martin Dawson

. . . .

ORPHAN: Jerusha Thacker

PARENT: Benjamin Thacker GUARDIAN: Tarlton Woodson

DATE: 5 Oct. 1803 AMOUNT OF BOND: $1,500

SECURITY: Goodman Barksdale

LOOSE BONDS, page 21

ORPHAN: John Jones
PARENT: James Jones   GUARDIAN: William R. Jones
DATE: 6 Dec. 1803   AMOUNT OF BOND: $6,000
SECURITY: Joshua Key

. . . .

ORPHAN: Jane Lewis Witt
PARENT: Lewis Witt   GUARDIAN: Thomas Montgomery
DATE: 2 Jan. 1804   AMOUNT OF BOND: $1,000
SECURITY: John Rife

. . . .

ORPHAN: Harmer Gilmer
PARENT: George Gilmer   GUARDIAN: George Gilmer
DATE: 3 Jan. 1804   AMOUNT OF BOND: $15,000
SECURITY: Francis Walker

. . . .

ORPHAN: Francis Gilmer
PARENT: George Gilmer   GUARDIAN: Charles Everett
DATE: 7 Feb. 1804   AMOUNT OF BOND: $5,000
SECURITY: George Divers

. . . .

ORPHAN: Lucy Gilmer
PARENT: George Gilmer   GUARDIAN: George Divers
DATE: 7 Feb. 1804   AMOUNT OF BOND: $5,000
SECURITY: Charles Everett

LOOSE BONDS, page 22

ORPHAN: Sarah Hudson

PARENT: John Hudson GUARDIAN: Charles A. Scott

DATE: 7 Feb. 1804 AMOUNT OF BOND: 1,000 pounds

SECURITY: Samuel Dyer
Craven Peyton

. . . .

ORPHAN: John W. Lewis

PARENT: John Lewis, Jr. GUARDIAN: Samuel Shelton

DATE: 6 Aug. 1804 AMOUNT OF BOND: $20,000

SECURITY: Samuel Dyer

. . . .

ORPHAN: Susannah F. Gilmer

PARENT: Doctor George Gilmer GUARDIAN: George Gilmer

DATE: 1 Oct. 1804 AMOUNT OF BOND: $15,000

SECURITY: W. D. Meriwether

. . . .

ORPHAN: Martha J., Lucy Ann, Virginia, Dabney, & Mary Jane Terril

PARENT: Richard Terril GUARDIAN: Isaac Miller

DATE: 1 Oct. 1804 AMOUNT OF BOND: $2,000

SECURITY: Dabney Carr, Peter Carr, Samuel Carr

. . . .

ORPHAN: Justiana[?] Burrus

PARENT: Charles Burrus [not deceased] GUARDIAN: William Frailey

DATE: 3 Dec. 1804 AMOUNT OF BOND: $2,000

SECURITY: Hancock Allen

Note: Justiana Burrus is further identified in the bond as a legatee of Thomas Ballard.

LOOSE BONDS, page 23

ORPHAN: Charles W., Samuel, Rachel J., & Elizabeth Hamner
PARENT: Elizabeth Hamner   GUARDIAN: Henly Hamner
DATE: 4 Feb. 1805   AMOUNT OF BOND: $1,000
SECURITY: Samuel Smithson

. . . .

ORPHAN: Jane Moore
PARENT: L[?]. R. Moore   GUARDIAN: Jacob Grass
DATE: 4 March 1805   AMOUNT OF BOND: $100
SECURITY: James Brooks

. . . .

ORPHAN: Asa Davis
PARENT: Benjamin Davis   GUARDIAN: Benjamin Davis
DATE: 2 Sept. 1805   AMOUNT OF BOND: 100 pounds
SECURITY: Joel Yancey

. . . .

ORPHAN: Charles Hudson
PARENT: John Hudson   GUARDIAN: John Hudson
DATE: 2 Dec. 1805   AMOUNT OF BOND: $6,000
SECURITY: John Harris

. . . .

LOOSE BONDS, page 24

ORPHAN: Wiley Dickenson
PARENT: Thomas Dickenson GUARDIAN: Elijah Watts
DATE: 6 Jan. 1806 AMOUNT OF BOND: $1,000
SECURITY: James Dickenson

. . . .

ORPHAN: Williamson Brown
PARENT: Andrew Brown GUARDIAN: Mary Brown
DATE: 3 Feb. 1806 AMOUNT OF BOND: $1,000
SECURITY: Joseph Sutherland

. . . .

ORPHAN: [Griffin?] Greffa, & Lucy Dickenson
PARENT: Thomas Dickenson GUARDIAN: Samuel Brockman
DATE: 3 Feb. 1806 AMOUNT OF BOND:
SECURITY: Ambrose Brockman

. . . .

ORPHAN: Betsey Carrell
PARENT: John Carrell GUARDIAN: Obediah Thomas
DATE: 3 Nov. 1806 AMOUNT OF BOND: 100 pounds
SECURITY: James Jopling

. . . .

ORPHAN: Hannah Shaver
PARENT: Frederick Shaver GUARDIAN: Charles Shaver
DATE: 4 Nov. 1806 AMOUNT OF BOND: $1,000
SECURITY: Achilles Durrett
John Rife

LOOSE BONDS, page 25

ORPHAN: Polly Spencer
PARENT: William Spencer   GUARDIAN: Henry Powell
DATE: 1 Dec. 1806   AMOUNT OF BOND: $100
SECURITY: Edmond Page

. . . .

ORPHAN: Lucy, & Griffin Dickenson
PARENT: Thomas Dickenson   GUARDIAN: Bernis Brown
DATE: 7 Jan. 1807   AMOUNT OF BOND: $1,000
SECURITY: James Dickenson

. . . .

ORPHAN: Sarah Shelton Foster
PARENT: James Foster   GUARDIAN: Alexander Roberts
DATE: 3 March 1807   AMOUNT OF BOND: $1,000
SECURITY: Sarah Shepherd,
Augustine Shepherd, Hudson Martin, Jr.

. . . .

ORPHAN: Susanna Foster
PARENT: James Foster   GUARDIAN: Sarah Shepherd
DATE: 3 March 1807   AMOUNT OF BOND: $1,000
SECURITY: Augustine Shepherd,
Weath^n Shelton, Alexander Roberts

. . . .

ORPHAN: William, & Christian Foster
PARENT: James Foster   GUARDIAN: William Woods
DATE: 4 March 1807   AMOUNT OF BOND: $2,000
SECURITY: Elijah Garth

LOOSE BONDS, page 26

ORPHAN: Peggy Draffen
PARENT: [none given]   GUARDIAN: Richard Hackley
DATE: 6 July 1807   AMOUNT OF BOND: $200
SECURITY: Joseph Bishop

. . . .

ORPHAN: Justian Burruss
PARENT: Charles Burruss   GUARDIAN: William Frailey
DATE: 7 Sept. 1807   AMOUNT OF BOND: $3,000
SECURITY: David Wood
          Parmenas Rogers

. . . .

ORPHAN: Cynthia, & Elizabeth Sneed
PARENT: Holeman Sneed   GUARDIAN: Clifton Garland
DATE: 7 Sept. 1807   AMOUNT OF BOND: $1,000
SECURITY: Rice Garland

. . . .

ORPHAN: Anne Cleveland
PARENT: Jeremiah Cleveland   GUARDIAN: Jeremiah Cleveland
DATE: 5 Oct. 1807   AMOUNT OF BOND: $1,000
SECURITY: Bernerd Franklin

. . . .

ORPHAN: Salley Cleveland
PARENT: Jeremiah Cleveland   GUARDIAN: James Watson
DATE: 5 Oct. 1807   AMOUNT OF BOND: $1,000
SECURITY: John Watson

LOOSE BONDS, page 27

ORPHAN: Jesse Grady
PARENT: Joshua Grady GUARDIAN: Joshua Grady
DATE: 6 Oct. 1807 AMOUNT OF BOND: $300
SECURITY: James Robinson, Philip Phillips, Richard Johnson, Charles C. Lacy

. . . .

ORPHAN: Shelton Farrar
PARENT: Richard Farrar GUARDIAN: Benjamin Harris
DATE: 2 Nov. 1807 AMOUNT OF BOND: $600
SECURITY: Chiles Terrell

. . . .

ORPHAN: Anne Moore
PARENT: Edward Moore GUARDIAN: John L. Moore
DATE: 5 Nov. 1807 AMOUNT OF BOND: $200
SECURITY: Peter Martin

. . . .

ORPHAN: George Booth
PARENT: George Booth GUARDIAN: Goodman Barksdale
DATE: 7 Dec. 1807 AMOUNT OF BOND: 100 pounds
SECURITY: Jonathan Barksdale

. . . .

ORPHAN: Franklin Buster
PARENT: Claudius Buster GUARDIAN: John Buster
DATE: 4 Jan. 1808 AMOUNT OF BOND: $1,000
SECURITY: William Shelton

LOOSE BONDS, page 28

ORPHAN: Lidy Jarrett
PARENT: Isham Jarrett   GUARDIAN: William Tuley, Jr.
DATE: 4 Jan. 1808   AMOUNT OF BOND: $300
SECURITY: William Tuley, Sr.

. . . .

ORPHAN: Elizabeth Strange
PARENT: Elizabeth Strange GUARDIAN: Samuel Powell
        [not deceased]
DATE: 9 March 1808   AMOUNT OF BOND: $1,000
SECURITY: James Old

. . . .

ORPHAN: Julia A. Brockman
PARENT: Samuel Brockman   GUARDIAN: Wiley Dickenson
DATE: 2 May 1808   AMOUNT OF BOND: $1,000
SECURITY: Ambrose Brockman

. . . .

ORPHAN: Mary Marks
PARENT: John M[arks]   GUARDIAN: John H. Marks
DATE: 2 May 1808   AMOUNT OF BOND: $10,000
SECURITY: Micajah Woods

. . . .

ORPHAN: Lucy M. Anderson
PARENT: Edmond Anderson   GUARDIAN: John H. Marks
DATE: 3 May 1808   AMOUNT OF BOND: $500
SECURITY: James H. Terrell

LOOSE BONDS, page 29

ORPHAN: Julia A. Brockman
PARENT: Samuel Brockman GUARDIAN: Wiley Dickenson
DATE: 6 May 1808 AMOUNT OF BOND: $1,000
SECURITY: Dabney Minor

....

ORPHAN: Peggy Lewis
PARENT: Thomas W. Lewis GUARDIAN: William D. Meriwether
DATE: 6 June 1808 AMOUNT OF BOND: $5,000
SECURITY: Alexander Garrett

....

ORPHAN: Ann Fitzhugh Nelson
PARENT: Robert Nelson GUARDIAN: Hugh Nelson
DATE: 6 June 1808 AMOUNT OF BOND: $2,000
SECURITY: John Walker

....

ORPHAN: John, & Wilson Mills
PARENT: Wyatt Mills GUARDIAN: John A. Michie
DATE: 3 Sept. 1808 AMOUNT OF BOND: $5,500
SECURITY: Joseph Mills
          Horsley Goodman

....

ORPHAN: Sims, Tandy, Blueford, Aggy, & Tazwell Brockman
PARENT: Samuel Brockman GUARDIAN: Anderson B. Carr
DATE: 3 Oct. 1808 AMOUNT OF BOND: 2,000 pounds
SECURITY: Drury Wood

LOOSE BONDS, page 30

ORPHAN: Sally Coles
PARENT: John Coles
GUARDIAN: Isaac A. Coles
DATE: 3 Oct. 1808
AMOUNT OF BOND: $15,000
SECURITY: Tucker Coles

. . . .

ORPHAN: Elizabeth, & Emily Coles
PARENT: John Coles
GUARDIAN: Tucker Coles
DATE: 3 Oct. 1808
AMOUNT OF BOND: $30,000
SECURITY: John[?] Coles
Isaac A. Coles

. . . .

ORPHAN: Elizabeth F. Mills
PARENT: Wyatt Mills
GUARDIAN: Edmond Davis
DATE: 3 Oct. 1808
AMOUNT OF BOND: $2,000
SECURITY: Robert Davis
Note from Salley Mills gives up right of guardianship to her daughter Elizabeth F. Mills

. . . .

ORPHAN: Polly Brown
PARENT: Andrew Brown
GUARDIAN: Anderson Brown
DATE: 7 Nov. 1808
AMOUNT OF BOND: $1,000
SECURITY: Martin Moore

. . . .

ORPHAN: James Allen
PARENT: Isaac Allen
GUARDIAN: James Allen
DATE: 8 Nov. 1808
AMOUNT OF BOND: $200
SECURITY: John Bibey
Benjamin Robinson

LOOSE BONDS, page 31

ORPHAN: Mary Slaughter
PARENT: John Slaughter GUARDIAN: John Slaughter
DATE: 6 Feb. 1809 AMOUNT OF BOND: $1,000
SECURITY: Thomas M. Randolph
Thomas Garth

. . . .

ORPHAN: Nancy Snead
PARENT: Holeman Snead GUARDIAN: John Waddy Lewis
DATE: 6 March 1809 AMOUNT OF BOND: $2,000
SECURITY: Robert Anderson

. . . .

ORPHAN: Parks Langford
PARENT: [none given] GUARDIAN: Richard N. Burton
DATE: 8 March 1809 AMOUNT OF BOND: $300
SECURITY: James Dudley

. . . .

ORPHAN: Robert L., & Waddy T. Slaughter
PARENT: John Slaughter GUARDIAN: James Scott
DATE: 10 March 1809 AMOUNT OF BOND: $3,000
SECURITY: John A. Michie

. . . .

ORPHAN: John H. Barksdale
PARENT: William Barksdale GUARDIAN: Nelson Barksdale
DATE: 5 June 1809 AMOUNT OF BOND: [not given]
SECURITY: Jonathan Barksdale

LOOSE BONDS, page 32

ORPHAN:	Jemima Gardner		
PARENT:	Nancy Gardner	GUARDIAN:	Samuel Woody
DATE:	8 Aug. 1809	AMOUNT OF BOND:	$100
SECURITY:	Samuel Wood		

. . . .

ORPHAN:	Susannah Gillum		
PARENT:	John Gillum	GUARDIAN:	Rebecca Gillum
DATE:	2 Oct. 1809	AMOUNT OF BOND:	$2,000
SECURITY:	Walter Key Joshua Key		

. . . .

ORPHAN:	Andrew Alexander		
PARENT:	John Alexander	GUARDIAN:	Charles Yancey
DATE:	6 Nov. 1809	AMOUNT OF BOND:	$1,000
SECURITY:	Jechonias Yancey		

. . . .

ORPHAN:	David, Fanny, Betsy, Garrett, Willis, Milly, Durrett, Walker, Cally, Nancy, & Henry Austin		
PARENT:	Henry Austin	GUARDIAN:	Nancy Austin
DATE:	6 Nov. 1809	AMOUNT OF BOND:	$3,000
SECURITY:	David Wood, James Early, Michael Catterton, Jacob Watts		

. . . .

ORPHAN:	John Mahanes		
PARENT:	Meredith Mahanes	GUARDIAN:	Lewis Mahanes
DATE:	6 Nov. 1809	AMOUNT OF BOND:	$500
SECURITY:	Samuel Mahanes		

LOOSE BONDS, page 33

ORPHAN: James Michie
PARENT: Patrick Michie   GUARDIAN: Horsley Goodman
DATE: 6 Nov. 1809   AMOUNT OF BOND: $1,000
SECURITY: John A. Michie

. . . .

ORPHAN: John Wheeler
PARENT: Robert Wheeler   GUARDIAN: William Woods
DATE: 6 Nov. 1809   AMOUNT OF BOND: $1,000
SECURITY: Tarlton Woodson

. . . .

ORPHAN: John F. Carr
PARENT: John Carr   GUARDIAN: Thomas D. Carr
DATE: 4 Dec. 1809   AMOUNT OF BOND: 1,600 pounds
SECURITY: Wiley Dickenson

. . . .

ORPHAN: Sally D. Carr
PARENT: John Carr   GUARDIAN: Thomas D. Carr
DATE: 4 Dec. 1809   AMOUNT OF BOND: 1,600 pounds
SECURITY: Wiley Dickenson

. . . .

ORPHAN: Polly M. Maupin
PARENT: John Maupin   GUARDIAN: [father] John Maupin (R H)
DATE: 3 April 1810   AMOUNT OF BOND: $500
SECURITY: James Jarman

LOOSE BONDS, page 34

ORPHAN: Emmerly Mahanes
PARENT: Meredeth Mahanes   GUARDIAN: Lewis Mahanes
DATE: 7 May 1810   AMOUNT OF BOND: $700
SECURITY: James Leake
William Johnson

. . . .

ORPHAN: Peter Schenk
PARENT: Cornelius Schenk   GUARDIAN: John Kelly
DATE: 7 May 1810   AMOUNT OF BOND: $2,000
SECURITY: William Watson

. . . .

ORPHAN: Polly, Aylett, Absolom W., & Jane Breedlove
PARENT: Madison Breedlove   GUARDIAN: William Smith (Sadler)
DATE: 3 Sept. 1810   AMOUNT OF BOND: 500 pounds
SECURITY: Dabney Minor,
Peter Minor, Samuel Carr

. . . .

ORPHAN: Sims, Tandy, Luford, Aggy, & Tazwell Brockman
PARENT: Samuel Brockman   GUARDIAN: Drury Wood
DATE: 3 Sept. 1810   AMOUNT OF BOND: $15,000
SECURITY: Thomas Carr

. . . .

ORPHAN: Susan Gillaspie
PARENT: Lewis Gillaspie   GUARDIAN: John Gillaspie
DATE: 3 Sept. 1810   AMOUNT OF BOND: $100
SECURITY: Samuel Garrison

LOOSE BONDS, page 35

ORPHAN: Nathaniel Anderson, Jr.
PARENT: Nathaniel Anderson, Sr. GUARDIAN: [father] Nathaniel Anderson, Sr.
DATE: 1 Oct. 1810 AMOUNT OF BOND: 500 pounds
SECURITY: William White
Samuel Shelton

. . . .

ORPHAN: Elizabeth Campbell
PARENT: Sylus Campbell GUARDIAN: John Campbell
DATE: 1 Oct. 1810 AMOUNT OF BOND: $300
SECURITY: Lewis Shiflett

. . . .

ORPHAN: Caty Norvell
PARENT: Benjamin Norvell GUARDIAN: Thomas Maxwell
DATE: 5 Nov. 1810 AMOUNT OF BOND: $1,000
SECURITY: John Norvell

. . . .

ORPHAN: Sarah Hamner
PARENT: John Hamner GUARDIAN: David Gentry
[not deceased]
DATE: 6 Nov. 1810 AMOUNT OF BOND: $500
SECURITY: James Old

. . . .

ORPHAN: Sarah Brown
PARENT: Bernard Brown GUARDIAN: Charles Brown
DATE: 3 Dec. 1810 AMOUNT OF BOND: $4,000
SECURITY: John Rodes
James Jarman

LOOSE BONDS, page 36

ORPHAN: John Gunter
PARENT: Austin Gunter GUARDIAN: William Weatherhead
DATE: 7 Jan. 1811 AMOUNT OF BOND: $1,000
SECURITY: James Dowell

. . . .

ORPHAN: Lydia Lewis
PARENT: Thomas W. Lewis GUARDIAN: William D. Meriwether
DATE: 5 Feb. 1811 AMOUNT OF BOND: $10,000
SECURITY: John M. Martin

. . . .

ORPHAN: Polly Lewis
PARENT: Thomas W. Lewis GUARDIAN: William D. Meriwether
DATE: 5 Feb. 1811 AMOUNT OF BOND: $10,000
SECURITY: John M. Martin

. . . .

ORPHAN: Kitty C., John M., & Lilburn R. Railey
PARENT: Martin Railey GUARDIAN: Elizabeth Railey
DATE: 6 May 1811 AMOUNT OF BOND: $10,000
SECURITY: Charles Railey
Randolph Railey

. . . .

ORPHAN: William Lewis Anderson
PARENT: Edmond Anderson GUARDIAN: John H. Marks
DATE: 5 Aug. 1811 AMOUNT OF BOND: $1,500
SECURITY: George Gilmer
Note of 4 May 1813 wants Henry Lindsay to show cause why William L. Anderson should not be removed from his apprenticeship.

LOOSE BONDS, page 37

ORPHAN: Lucy Ann Terrell
PARENT: Richard Terrell GUARDIAN: Dabney Carr
DATE: 6 Aug. 1811 AMOUNT OF BOND: 2,000 pounds
SECURITY: Alexander Garrett

. . . .

ORPHAN: Jane Rice
PARENT: Holeman Rice GUARDIAN: James Boyd
DATE: 2 Sept. 1811 AMOUNT OF BOND: $1,000
SECURITY: Mask[?] Leake

. . . .

ORPHAN: John, Frances, & Peggy Mills
PARENT: Menan Mills GUARDIAN: Micajah Woods
[not deceased?]
DATE: 3 Sept. 1811 AMOUNT OF BOND: $1,500
SECURITY: Clifton Rodes

. . . .

ORPHAN: William Mills
PARENT: Menan Mills GUARDIAN: Clifton Rodes
[not deceased?]
DATE: 3 Sept. 1811 AMOUNT OF BOND: $500
SECURITY: Micajah Woods

. . . .

ORPHAN: Mathew C., Mary A., Sophia, Skiler, & Francis Harris
PARENT: Skiler Harris GUARDIAN: Hawes Coleman
DATE: 4 Nov. 1811 AMOUNT OF BOND: $10,000
SECURITY: Andrew Hart

LOOSE BONDS, page 38

ORPHAN: Samuel H. Moon
PARENT: Jacob Moon GUARDIAN: Richard Moon, Sr.
DATE: 4 Nov. 1811 AMOUNT OF BOND: $2,000
SECURITY: Littleberry Moon

. . . .

ORPHAN: Polly Wingfield
PARENT: Edward Wingfield GUARDIAN: Larkin Hudson
DATE: 4 Nov. 1811 AMOUNT OF BOND: $1,000
SECURITY: Anderson Harris
Mathew Wingfield

. . . .

ORPHAN: Catharine Railey
PARENT: Martin Railey GUARDIAN: Anderson Shiflett
DATE: 5 Nov. 1811 AMOUNT OF BOND: $2,000
SECURITY: Joel Shiflett

. . . .

ORPHAN: Dicy Myers
PARENT: Christopher Myers GUARDIAN: Thomas Suddarth
DATE: 6 Nov. 1811 AMOUNT OF BOND: $2,000
SECURITY: John Randal
James Dowell

. . . .

ORPHAN: Skiler Moon
PARENT: Jacob Moon GUARDIAN: Littleberry Moon
DATE: 2 Dec. 1811 AMOUNT OF BOND: $4,000
SECURITY: William Moon

LOOSE BONDS, page 39

ORPHAN: George Ballard
PARENT: Edward Ballard   GUARDIAN: [father] Edward Ballard
DATE: 6 Jan. 1812   AMOUNT OF BOND: $500
SECURITY: John Ballard

. . . .

ORPHAN: Robert Bishop
PARENT: [none given]   GUARDIAN: Isham Chisholm
DATE: 6 Jan. 1812   AMOUNT OF BOND: $200
SECURITY: Joseph Bernard

. . . .

ORPHAN: Daniel Railey
PARENT: Martin Railey   GUARDIAN: Elizabeth Railey
DATE: 6 Jan. 1812   AMOUNT OF BOND: $2,000
SECURITY: Joel Shiflett

. . . .

ORPHAN: John Scott
PARENT: John Scott   GUARDIAN: Samuel Shelton
DATE: 3 Aug. 1812   AMOUNT OF BOND: $20,000
SECURITY: Samuel Dyer
          Christopher Hudson

. . . .

ORPHAN: Nelson K. Eubank
PARENT: George Eubank   GUARDIAN: John Eubank
DATE: 7 Sept. 1812   AMOUNT OF BOND: $2,000
SECURITY: Jesse P. Key

LOOSE BONDS, page 40

ORPHAN: Jeremiah, & Siotha Gillum
PARENT: Bennett Gillum   GUARDIAN: Elisha Sowell
DATE: 7 Sept. 1812   AMOUNT OF BOND: $1,000
SECURITY: James B. Watson

. . . .

ORPHAN: Patsy Grayson
PARENT: Thomas Grayson   GUARDIAN: Joseph Field
DATE: 7 Sept. 1812   AMOUNT OF BOND: $1,000
SECURITY: William Wood

. . . .

ORPHAN: Martha, & Elizabeth Burrus
PARENT: Isaac Burrus   GUARDIAN: Hawkey Ferguson
DATE: 5 Oct. 1812   AMOUNT OF BOND: $500
SECURITY: Wiley Ferguson

. . . .

ORPHAN: Henly, Sarah, John, & George Carr
PARENT: Micajah Carr   GUARDIAN: David Carr
DATE: 5 Oct. 1812   AMOUNT OF BOND: $6,000
SECURITY: Jesse P. Key
          Zachariah Shackelford

. . . .

ORPHAN: Jane, Fanny, & Benjamin Sandridge
PARENT: Joshua Sandridge   GUARDIAN: Susannah Sandridge
DATE: 3 Nov. 1812   AMOUNT OF BOND: $2,000
SECURITY: Crenshaw White

LOOSE BONDS, page 41

ORPHAN: Polly Wood
PARENT: Anne Wood   GUARDIAN: William Grymes
DATE: 7 Dec. 1812   AMOUNT OF BOND: $100
SECURITY: Henry Wood

. . . .

ORPHAN: Sally C. Norvell
PARENT: Benjamin Norvell   GUARDIAN: Robert B. Maxwell
DATE: 4 Jan. 1813   AMOUNT OF BOND: $2,000
SECURITY: Jesse P. Key
          Thomas Maxwell

. . . .

ORPHAN: Nathaniel Anderson
PARENT: Nathaniel Anderson   GUARDIAN: Christopher Hudson
DATE: 5 Jan. 1813   AMOUNT OF BOND: $5,000
SECURITY: Charles Yancey

. . . .

ORPHAN: Jane Carr
PARENT: John Carr   GUARDIAN: [father] John Carr
DATE: 5 Jan. 1813   AMOUNT OF BOND: $100
SECURITY: John M. Martin

. . . .

ORPHAN: Sally Key Eubank
PARENT: George Eubank   GUARDIAN: John Eubank, Sr.
DATE: 1 March 1813   AMOUNT OF BOND: $2,000
SECURITY: Tandy Key

LOOSE BONDS, page 42

ORPHAN: Edmond Harris
PARENT: William Harris   GUARDIAN: Daniel Maupin
DATE: 2 March 1813   AMOUNT OF BOND: $500
SECURITY: William Jameson

. . . .

ORPHAN: Sarah, William, & Milly Durrett
PARENT: James Durrett   GUARDIAN: [father] James Durrett
DATE: 6 April 1813   AMOUNT OF BOND: $1,000
SECURITY: Marshall Durrett

. . . .

ORPHAN: Nancy Moore
PARENT: William Moore   GUARDIAN: Claybourn Gentry
DATE: 3 May 1813   AMOUNT OF BOND: $100
SECURITY: Jesse P. Key

. . . .

ORPHAN: Sarah Thomason
PARENT: Abias Thomason   GUARDIAN: Benjamin Gillock
DATE: 7 June 1813   AMOUNT OF BOND: $200
SECURITY: Robert Gillock
          William Hogg

. . . .

ORPHAN: Nancy, John, & Marbell Camden
PARENT: Marbell Camden   GUARDIAN: Sarah Camden
DATE: 5 July 1813   AMOUNT OF BOND: $1,000
SECURITY: Thomas Hunton

LOOSE BONDS, page 43

ORPHAN: Patsey Lively

PARENT: Sally Curry
[not deceased]

GUARDIAN: James Dudley

DATE: 2 Aug. 1813

AMOUNT OF BOND: $150

SECURITY: Parks B. Landford

. . . .

ORPHAN: Mary L., Elizabeth Ann, Robert James, & Dorothy Moorman

PARENT: Robert Moorman

GUARDIAN: Dorothy Moorman

DATE: 2 Aug. 1813

AMOUNT OF BOND: $7,000

SECURITY: Benjamin Johnson
John Harris

. . . .

ORPHAN: Washington Patrick

PARENT: John Patrick

GUARDIAN: [father] John Patrick

DATE: 2 Aug. 1813

AMOUNT OF BOND: $500

SECURITY: John Buster

. . . .

ORPHAN: Elizabeth, & Harriet Smith

PARENT: Joel Smith

GUARDIAN: Charles Patrick

DATE: 2 Aug. 1813

AMOUNT OF BOND: $4,000

SECURITY: William Ramsey,
Thomas McCullock, John Patrick

. . . .

ORPHAN: Sarah Grayson

PARENT: Thomas Grayson

GUARDIAN: Ralph H. Field

DATE: 6 Sept. 1813

AMOUNT OF BOND: $1,500

SECURITY: Benjamin Martin
John Wood

LOOSE BONDS, page 44

ORPHAN: Nancy W. Old
PARENT: John Old GUARDIAN: Thomas Eubank
DATE: 6 Sept. 1813 AMOUNT OF BOND: $3,000
SECURITY: James Eubank
Gideon Carr

. . . .

ORPHAN: Malinda W. Martin
PARENT: George Martin GUARDIAN: William Woods (S)[Survey
DATE: 4 Oct. 1813 AMOUNT OF BOND: $10,000
SECURITY: Micajah Woods

. . . .

ORPHAN: Nathaniel Hays
PARENT: James Hays, Sr. GUARDIAN: James Hays, Jr.
DATE: 1 Nov. 1813 AMOUNT OF BOND: $2,000
SECURITY: Thomas Martin
John Hays

. . . .

ORPHAN: Bennett D. Ballard
PARENT: Bland Ballard GUARDIAN: Garland Ballard
DATE: 6 Dec. 1813 AMOUNT OF BOND: $750
SECURITY: Thomas Burton

. . . .

ORPHAN: Thomas Harris
PARENT: William Harris GUARDIAN: William Jameson
DATE: 6 Dec. 1813 AMOUNT OF BOND: $1,00
SECURITY: Daniel Maupin

LOOSE BONDS, page 45

ORPHAN: Larkin Harris
PARENT: William Harris GUARDIAN: Daniel Maupin
DATE: 6 Dec. 1813 AMOUNT OF BOND: $1,000
SECURITY: William Jameson

. . . .

ORPHAN: Polly, William, Benajah, George, Mores, & Margaret Walters
PARENT: Joseph Walters GUARDIAN: Nicholas Gentry
       [not deceased]
DATE: 6 Dec. 1813 AMOUNT OF BOND: $500
SECURITY: James Old
       Alexander Garrett

. . . .

ORPHAN: James Old Walters
PARENT: Joseph Walters GUARDIAN: Nicholas Gentry
       [not deceased]
DATE: 6 Dec. 1813 AMOUNT OF BOND: $1,000
SECURITY: James Old
       Alexander Garrett

. . . .

ORPHAN: James, & William Watson
PARENT: Richard P. Watson GUARDIAN: Thomas Cobbs
DATE: 6 Dec. 1813 AMOUNT OF BOND: $2,000
SECURITY: William Suddarth

. . . .

ORPHAN: George W. Catlett
PARENT: Kemp Catlett GUARDIAN: William Watson
DATE: 3 Jan. 1814 AMOUNT OF BOND: $500
SECURITY: William Stevens

LOOSE BONDS, page 46

ORPHAN: John Darneille
PARENT: Isaac Darneille GUARDIAN: John Harris
DATE: 3 Jan. 1814 AMOUNT OF BOND: $3,000
SECURITY: Alexander Garrett

. . . .

ORPHAN: Lucinda, & Andlyenly[?] Watson
PARENT: Richard P. Watson GUARDIAN: Thomas Cobbs
DATE: 3 Jan. 1814 AMOUNT OF BOND: $3,000
SECURITY: Charles Yancey

. . . .

ORPHAN: Francis Burnley
PARENT: James Burnley GUARDIAN: Ann Burnley
DATE: 7 Feb. 1814 AMOUNT OF BOND: $1,000
SECURITY: Joseph Bishop

. . . .

ORPHAN: Thomas K. Catlett
PARENT: Kemp Catlett GUARDIAN: John M. Perry
DATE: 7 Feb. 1814 AMOUNT OF BOND: $150
SECURITY: Dabney Minor

. . . .

ORPHAN: Mary Hunt
PARENT: Benjamin Hunt GUARDIAN: James Eubank
DATE: 7 Feb. 1814 AMOUNT OF BOND: $700
SECURITY: Thomas Eubank

LOOSE BONDS, page 47

ORPHAN: Morris Moore
PARENT: Richard Moore   GUARDIAN: John Rife
DATE: 7 Feb. 1814   AMOUNT OF BOND: $500
SECURITY: Joseph Coffman

. . . .

ORPHAN: James, & William Watson
PARENT: Richard P. Watson   GUARDIAN: Martha Watson
DATE: 7 Feb. 1814   AMOUNT OF BOND: $1,000
SECURITY: John Brown

. . . .

ORPHAN: Isaac Hays
PARENT: James Hays   GUARDIAN: Robert Brooks
DATE: 7 March 1814   AMOUNT OF BOND: $1,500
SECURITY: George M. Woods

. . . .

ORPHAN: Thomas Hays
PARENT: James Hays   GUARDIAN: Robert Brooks
DATE: 7 March 1814   AMOUNT OF BOND: $2,000
SECURITY: George M. Woods

. . . .

ORPHAN: Susanna Travillian
PARENT: Thomas Travillian   GUARDIAN: Benjamin Thurmond
DATE: 7 March 1814   AMOUNT OF BOND: $4,000
SECURITY: Mecham Carr

LOOSE BONDS, page 48

ORPHAN: Nancy Day
PARENT: Polly Day GUARDIAN: Joshua Riley
DATE: 10 March 1814 AMOUNT OF BOND: $100
SECURITY: William Booth

. . . .

ORPHAN: Elizabeth Moore
PARENT: William Moore GUARDIAN: John Gillum
DATE: 2 May 1814 AMOUNT OF BOND: $200
SECURITY: John Moyer

. . . .

ORPHAN: Lucinda, & Anleonia[?] Watson
PARENT: Richard P. Watson GUARDIAN: Samuel L. Hart
DATE: 7 June 1814 AMOUNT OF BOND: $2,000
SECURITY: Edmund Anderson

. . . .

ORPHAN: Elizabeth Clarkson
PARENT: David Clarkson GUARDIAN: John Watson (L M) [Littl
DATE: 3 Oct. 1814 AMOUNT OF BOND: $5,000 Mounta
SECURITY: Drury Wood

. . . .

ORPHAN: Nancy Clarkson
PARENT: David Clarkson GUARDIAN: John Watson (L M) [Littl
DATE: 3 Oct. 1814 AMOUNT OF BOND: $5,000 Mount
SECURITY: Drury Wood

LOOSE BONDS, page 49

ORPHAN: Elizabeth Clarkson
PARENT: Julius Clarkson   GUARDIAN: Jesse Lewis
DATE: 3 Oct. 1814   AMOUNT OF BOND: $12,000
SECURITY: Alexander Garrett

. . . .

ORPHAN: Ann Robertson
PARENT: William Robertson   GUARDIAN: Rice Smith
DATE: 3 Oct. 1814   AMOUNT OF BOND: $1,000
SECURITY: William Leake

. . . .

ORPHAN: Nelson Travillian
PARENT: Thomas Travillian   GUARDIAN: James Travillian
DATE: 3 Oct. 1814   AMOUNT OF BOND: $3,000
SECURITY: John Watson (L M)
           [Little Mountain]

. . . .

ORPHAN: Ann Patience, Thomas J., & George W. Old
PARENT: John Old   GUARDIAN: James Old
DATE: 7 Nov. 1814   AMOUNT OF BOND: $1,000
SECURITY: William Woods (S)
           [Surveyor?]

. . . .

ORPHAN: Hudson Fretwell
PARENT: William Fretwell   GUARDIAN: William Brown
DATE: 1 Jan. 1815   AMOUNT OF BOND: $5,000
SECURITY: Bezaleel Brown

LOOSE BONDS, page 50

ORPHAN: Nicholas, John, Daniel, James, Sarah, & Ross Drumheller
PARENT: Jacob Drumheller GUARDIAN: James Old
DATE: 5 Jan. 1815 AMOUNT OF BOND: $500
SECURITY: John Watson

. . . .

ORPHAN: Nancy Herrard
PARENT: Voluntine Herrard GUARDIAN: Edward H. Gladden
DATE: 6 Feb. 1815 AMOUNT OF BOND: $100
SECURITY: Jesse W. Garth, William D. Fitch, Alexander Garrett

. . . .

ORPHAN: Elizabeth L. W. Martin
PARENT: George Martin GUARDIAN: James Woods
DATE: 6 Feb. 1815 AMOUNT OF BOND: $3,000
SECURITY: George M. Woods
Jesse W. Garth

. . . .

ORPHAN: Elizabeth, & Ann Townley
PARENT: Mann Townley GUARDIAN: David J. Lewis
[not deceased]
DATE: 6 Feb. 1815 AMOUNT OF BOND: $3,000
SECURITY: Dabney Minor

. . . .

ORPHAN: Tandy, Bluford, Aggy, & Tazwell Brockman
PARENT: Samuel Brockman GUARDIAN: Sims Brockman
DATE: 6 March 1815 AMOUNT OF BOND: $10,000
SECURITY: Wiley Dickenson

LOOSE BONDS, page 51

ORPHAN: William Watson
PARENT: Richard P. Watson   GUARDIAN: Martha Watson
DATE: 6 March 1815   AMOUNT OF BOND: $1,000
SECURITY: Charles Yancey

. . . .

ORPHAN: Benjamin, & Robert Wheeler
PARENT: Robert Wheeler   GUARDIAN: Micajah Wheeler
DATE: 6 March 1815   AMOUNT OF BOND: $500
SECURITY: Pleasant Gillum

. . . .

ORPHAN: Catharine Goodridge
PARENT: John Goodridge   GUARDIAN: James Burton
DATE: 1 May 1815   AMOUNT OF BOND: $2,400
SECURITY: Wiley Dickenson

. . . .

ORPHAN: Virginia Terrell
PARENT: Richard Terrell   GUARDIAN: Samuel Carr
DATE: 1 May 1815   AMOUNT OF BOND: $40,000
SECURITY: Jonathan B. Carr

. . . .

ORPHAN: Lucy Rice
PARENT: Holeman Rice   GUARDIAN: Woodson P. Clarke
DATE: 5 June 1815   AMOUNT OF BOND: $100
SECURITY: William Leake

LOOSE BONDS, page 52

ORPHAN: William, Oliver, & Benajah Cleveland
PARENT: Jeremiah Cleveland   GUARDIAN: Jeremiah Cleveland
DATE: 7 Aug. 1815   AMOUNT OF BOND: $3,000
SECURITY: Benjamin Sowell

. . . .

ORPHAN: Malinda Roberts
PARENT: Richard Roberts   GUARDIAN: James Roberts
DATE: 7 Aug. 1815   AMOUNT OF BOND: $2,000
SECURITY: Frederick Gillum

. . . .

ORPHAN: John, & Joseph F. Wingfield
PARENT: Edward Wingfield   GUARDIAN: Nancy Wingfield
DATE: 7 Aug. 1815   AMOUNT OF BOND: $2,000
SECURITY: Christopher Wingfield
           Reuben Wingfield

. . . .

ORPHAN: Thomas West
PARENT: James H. West   GUARDIAN: Robert Brooks
DATE: 4 Sept. 1815   AMOUNT OF BOND: $5,000
SECURITY: William Woods (S)
           [Surveyor]

. . . .

ORPHAN: Nancy, Eliza, & Abram Munday
PARENT: Abram Munday   GUARDIAN: John Price
DATE: 2 Oct. 1815   AMOUNT OF BOND: $5,000
SECURITY: Nicholas Hall

LOOSE BONDS, page 53

ORPHAN:	Abram, Frederick, Charles, Surberry, John, Elizabeth, & George Shaffer
PARENT:	John Shaffer
GUARDIAN:	[father] John Shaffer
DATE:	2 Oct. 1815
AMOUNT OF BOND:	$500
SECURITY:	James Old

. . . .

ORPHAN: Margaret Brown [age 15 years]
PARENT: Andrew Brown   GUARDIAN: [brother] John Brown
DATE: 6 Nov. 1815   AMOUNT OF BOND: $4,000
SECURITY: William Woods (S) [Surveyor]

. . . .

ORPHAN: Mary Downs [Douris?]
PARENT: John McBridee   GUARDIAN: Thomas Johnson
DATE: 4 Dec. 1815   AMOUNT OF BOND: $100
SECURITY: John Craddock

. . . .

ORPHAN: Joseph S. Leake
PARENT: Austin Leake   GUARDIAN: Samuel Leake
DATE: 4 Dec. 1815   AMOUNT OF BOND: $2,000
SECURITY: William Leake

. . . .

ORPHAN: Mary Fry
PARENT: Reubin Fry   GUARDIAN: Mathew Maury
DATE: 4 Dec. 1815   AMOUNT OF BOND: $1,000
SECURITY: Francis F. Maury

LOOSE BONDS, page 54

ORPHAN: Isabella, & Jane Maxwell
PARENT: John Maxwell   GUARDIAN: Andrew Squair[?]
DATE: 4 Dec. 1815   AMOUNT OF BOND: $4,000
SECURITY: Christopher Hudson

. . . .

ORPHAN: Jefferson Smith
PARENT: Joel Smith   GUARDIAN: John Wallace
DATE: 5 Feb. 1816   AMOUNT OF BOND: $2,000
SECURITY: Benjamin Davis
          Benjamin Hardin

. . . .

ORPHAN: James, & Samuel Winns
PARENT: Samuel Winns   GUARDIAN: [father] Samuel Winns
DATE: 5 Feb. 1816   AMOUNT OF BOND: $1,500
SECURITY: Crenshaw Fretwell

. . . .

ORPHAN: Patsey, Debora, Jane, & Patterson Winns
PARENT: Samuel Winns   GUARDIAN: [father] Samuel Winns
DATE: 4 March 1816   AMOUNT OF BOND: $1,200
SECURITY: Garland Garth

. . . .

ORPHAN: Mary Ann, & Nancy Lewis
PARENT: Jane Lewis   GUARDIAN: John Kelly
DATE: 7 March 1816   AMOUNT OF BOND: $500
SECURITY: Alexander Garrett

LOOSE BONDS, page 55

ORPHAN: Richard W. Brooks
PARENT: James Brooks   GUARDIAN: Charles Yancey
DATE: 1 May 1815   AMOUNT OF BOND: $5,000
SECURITY: Ralph H. Yancey, Joseph Coffman, Jechonias Yancey

. . . .

ORPHAN: Julius W., John N., William L., & Arramintha W. Clarkson
PARENT: Reuben Clarkson   GUARDIAN: [father] Reuben Clarkson
DATE: 3 June 1816   AMOUNT OF BOND: $2,000
SECURITY: David J. Lewis
Manoah Clarkson

. . . .

ORPHAN: Fleet Goodridge
PARENT: John Goodridge   GUARDIAN: Lucy Goodridge
DATE: 3 June 1816   AMOUNT OF BOND: $5,000
SECURITY: James Burton

. . . .

ORPHAN: James, Mary Ann, & Thomas Martin
PARENT: Cary Martin   GUARDIAN: Henry Pemberton
DATE: 2 Sept. 1816   AMOUNT OF BOND: $1,000
SECURITY: William Suddarth

. . . .

ORPHAN: Thomas, & John Salmon
PARENT: John D. Salmon   GUARDIAN: James Duke
DATE: 4 Sept. 1815   AMOUNT OF BOND: $5,000
SECURITY: Thomas Salmon
Joel Foster

LOOSE BONDS, page 56

ORPHAN: Nancy Marrs
PARENT: John Marrs GUARDIAN: Wilson Roberts
DATE: 7 Oct. 1816 AMOUNT OF BOND: $1,000
SECURITY: John Jones

. . . .

ORPHAN: Sopha, Jane, & Hugh Rice Morris
PARENT: Jacob Morris GUARDIAN: John Morris
DATE: 7 Oct. 1816 AMOUNT OF BOND: $12,000
SECURITY: Jacob Morris
Erasmus Stribling

. . . .

ORPHAN: Susan Colvin
PARENT: Alexander Colvin GUARDIAN: Jacob C. Lupton
DATE: 4 Nov. 1816 AMOUNT OF BOND: $50
SECURITY: Samuel Ritter

. . . .

ORPHAN: Jane Breedlove
PARENT: Madison Breedlove GUARDIAN: Oliver Cleaveland
DATE: 2 Dec. 1816 AMOUNT OF BOND: $1,000
SECURITY: Nimrod Bramham

. . . .

ORPHAN: Mary Frances Cobbs
PARENT: Samuel Cobbs GUARDIAN: [father] Samuel Cobbs
DATE: 2 Dec. 1816 AMOUNT OF BOND: $1,000
SECURITY: Francis McGehee

LOOSE BONDS, page 57

ORPHAN: Susannah, Mildred, Sarah Rosanna, & Polly Nailor
PARENT: Thomas Nailor   GUARDIAN: [father] Thomas Nailor
DATE: 6 Jan. 1817   AMOUNT OF BOND: $2,000
SECURITY: Matthew P. Watson

. . . .

ORPHAN: Frances Jarman Mullins
PARENT: John Mullins, Jr.   GUARDIAN: James Jarman
DATE: 3 Feb. 1817   AMOUNT OF BOND: $4,000
SECURITY: John Rodes

. . . .

ORPHAN: Mary Appleberry
PARENT: John Appleberry   GUARDIAN: Dabney Carr
DATE: 3 March 1817   AMOUNT OF BOND: $4,000
SECURITY: William Appleberry

. . . .

ORPHAN: Julius W., John N., William L., & Arramintha W. Clarkson
PARENT: Reuben Clarkson   GUARDIAN: [father] Reuben Clarkson
DATE: 3 March 1817   AMOUNT OF BOND: $4,000
SECURITY: Samuel L. Hart
          Jeremiah A. Goodman

. . . .

ORPHAN: Anne Dickerson
PARENT: John Dickerson   GUARDIAN: Brice Edwards
DATE: 3 March 1817   AMOUNT OF BOND: $4,000
SECURITY: John Douglass

LOOSE BONDS, page 58

ORPHAN: William, & James Hurt
PARENT: William Hurt   GUARDIAN: James Hurt
DATE: 3 March 1817   AMOUNT OF BOND: $500
SECURITY: James Dudley
            Thomas Carter

. . . .

ORPHAN: Nathaniel, & Robert Garland
PARENT: Anderson Garland   GUARDIAN: John Hays
DATE: 8 April 1817   AMOUNT OF BOND: $1,500
SECURITY: William Ramsey

. . . .

ORPHAN: James West
PARENT: James H. West   GUARDIAN: Thomas West
DATE: 8 April 1817   AMOUNT OF BOND: $4,000
SECURITY: John Hays
            Jechonias Yancey

. . . .

ORPHAN: Patsey Mills
PARENT: James Mills   GUARDIAN: [father] James Mills
DATE: 6 July 1817   AMOUNT OF BOND: $200
SECURITY: Jesse Garth

. . . .

ORPHAN: Harriet Scipe
PARENT: Michael Scipe   GUARDIAN: Tucker Coles
DATE: 7 July 1817   AMOUNT OF BOND: $1,000
SECURITY: Isaac A. Coles

LOOSE BONDS, page 59

ORPHAN: William Watson
PARENT: Richard P. Watson   GUARDIAN: Samuel L. Hart
DATE: 1 Sept. 1817   AMOUNT OF BOND: $5,000
SECURITY: George M. Woods

. . . .

ORPHAN: Burnett D. Ballard
PARENT: Bland Ballard   GUARDIAN: Garland Ballard
DATE: 6 Oct. 1817   AMOUNT OF BOND: $150
SECURITY: Horsley Goodman

. . . .

ORPHAN: Elizabeth Durrett
PARENT: John Durrett   GUARDIAN: Price Key
DATE: 3 Nov. 1817   AMOUNT OF BOND: $20,000
SECURITY: Nelson Barksdale
           Davis Durrett

. . . .

ORPHAN: Sarah Durrett
PARENT: John Durrett   GUARDIAN: Price Key
DATE: 3 Nov. 1817   AMOUNT OF BOND: $20,000
SECURITY: Nelson Barksdale
           Davis Durrett

. . . .

ORPHAN: Thomas, Isaac, Matilda, & Richard Durrett
PARENT: John D. Durrett   GUARDIAN: Francis Durrett
DATE: 1 Dec. 1817   AMOUNT OF BOND: $20,000
SECURITY: Davis Durrett
           Isaac Davis, Jr.

LOOSE BONDS, page 60

ORPHAN:	Elizabeth M. Jarman		
PARENT:	William Jarman	GUARDIAN:	James Jarman
DATE:	1 Dec. 1817	AMOUNT OF BOND:	$2,000
SECURITY:	William Woods (S) [Surveyor]		

. . . .

ORPHAN:	Jesse Miller		
PARENT:	Polly Miller	GUARDIAN:	Samuel Wood
DATE:	1 Dec. 1817	AMOUNT OF BOND:	$150
SECURITY:	John Dollins		

. . . .

ORPHAN:	John Davis		
PARENT:	Jacob Davis	GUARDIAN:	Samuel Irvin
DATE:	5 Jan. 1818	AMOUNT OF BOND:	$2,000
SECURITY:	Henry T. Harris		

. . . .

ORPHAN:	Susan Speace		
PARENT:	Jacob Speace	GUARDIAN:	James Brooks
DATE:	5 Jan. 1818	AMOUNT OF BOND:	$3,000
SECURITY:	John Burger		

. . . .

ORPHAN:	William Spencer		
PARENT:	William Spencer	GUARDIAN:	John Pleasants
DATE:	5 Jan. 1818	AMOUNT OF BOND:	$100
SECURITY:	Nathaniel Thacker		

LOOSE BONDS, page 61

ORPHAN: Elizabeth Lewis
PARENT: Thomas W. Lewis   GUARDIAN: Nicholas H. Lewis
DATE: 2 Feb. 1818   AMOUNT OF BOND: $6,000
SECURITY: Samuel O. Minor

. . . .

ORPHAN: Morning[?] Hart Walton
PARENT: [none given]   GUARDIAN: Thomas Naylor
DATE: 3 Aug. 1818   AMOUNT OF BOND: $400
SECURITY: Mathew P. Walton

. . . .

ORPHAN: Celia Martin
PARENT: Elisha Martin   GUARDIAN: Uriah K. Yancey
DATE: 7 Sept. 1818   AMOUNT OF BOND: $100
SECURITY: William H. Martin

. . . .

ORPHAN: William Mathews
PARENT: Charles Mathews   GUARDIAN: Hannah Proctor
DATE: 7 Sept. 1818   AMOUNT OF BOND: $100
SECURITY: Isaiah Stout

. . . .

ORPHAN: Joshua Abell
PARENT: Caleb S. Abell   GUARDIAN: Benjamin Martin
DATE: 5 Oct. 1818   AMOUNT OF BOND: $5,000
SECURITY: George M. Woods

LOOSE BONDS, page 62

ORPHAN: Mary Elizabeth, Thomas, Jane Turner, & Anna M. Barclay
PARENT: Robert Barclay GUARDIAN: John Harris
DATE: 5 Oct. 1818 AMOUNT OF BOND: $10,000
SECURITY: Alexander Garrett
Marshall Durrett

. . . .

ORPHAN: Elizabeth Brown
PARENT: Bernis Brown GUARDIAN: Charles Carthra[?]
DATE: 5 Oct. 1818 AMOUNT OF BOND: $6,000
SECURITY: Bernis Brown

. . . .

ORPHAN: Polly, Elisha, William, & Amanda Browning
PARENT: Jonathan Browning GUARDIAN: Jonathan Browning
DATE: 5 Oct. 1818 AMOUNT OF BOND: $5,000
SECURITY: Goodman Barksdale
Samuel Barksdale

. . . .

ORPHAN: Winney, Anny, & Susannah Browning
PARENT: Jonathan Browning GUARDIAN: Jonathan Browning
DATE: 5 Oct. 1818 AMOUNT OF BOND: $5,000
SECURITY: Goodman Barksdale
Samuel Barksdale

. . . .

ORPHAN: Martha Loving
PARENT: Randolph Loving GUARDIAN: Eli Noel
DATE: 2 Nov. 1818 AMOUNT OF BOND: $500
SECURITY: Garland Mallory

LOOSE BONDS, page 63

ORPHAN: Eliza Walker
PARENT: Patsey Walker   GUARDIAN: Phillip Phillips
DATE: 4 Nov. 1818   AMOUNT OF BOND: $300
SECURITY: George W. Kinsolving

. . . .

ORPHAN: Nancy Mullins
PARENT: Anthony Mullins   GUARDIAN: George Pace
DATE: 5 Nov. 1818   AMOUNT OF BOND: $100
SECURITY: Charles Lively

. . . .

ORPHAN: James D. Allen
PARENT: Richard H. Allen GUARDIAN: James O. Carr
DATE: 7 Dec. 1818   AMOUNT OF BOND: $12,000
SECURITY: Dabney Minor

. . . .

ORPHAN: Martha Appleberry
PARENT: John Appleberry   GUARDIAN: Samuel W. Harris
DATE: 7 Dec. 1818   AMOUNT OF BOND: $6,000
SECURITY: William A. Harris
          William Elsom

. . . .

ORPHAN: James, & Mary Ann Mildred Dossey
PARENT: James Dossey   GUARDIAN: Richard Dossey
DATE: 1 Jan. 1819   AMOUNT OF BOND: $1,200
SECURITY: Edmund Davis
          Isaac Sims

LOOSE BONDS, page 64

ORPHAN: Ann E. Anderson
PARENT: Edmund Anderson   GUARDIAN: Francis McGehee
DATE: 1 Feb. 1819   AMOUNT OF BOND: $1,000
SECURITY: Henry White

. . . .

ORPHAN: Elijah, Kelly, Eliza, & Nancy Garrison
PARENT: James Garrison   GUARDIAN: Achilles Garrison
DATE: 1 Feb. 1819   AMOUNT OF BOND: $100
SECURITY: Mathew Rodes

. . . .

ORPHAN: Patsey Marshall
PARENT: Polly Marshall   GUARDIAN: Thomas Marshall
DATE: 2 March 1819   AMOUNT OF BOND: $2,500
SECURITY: John Dickenson

. . . .

ORPHAN: Rachel, & Polly Carr
PARENT: Mechans Carr   GUARDIAN: Bernard Carr
DATE: 7 June 1819   AMOUNT OF BOND: $1,500
SECURITY: John Rothwell

. . . .

ORPHAN: Eliza Johnson
PARENT: Benjamin Johnson   GUARDIAN: Fleming Johnson
DATE: 7 June 1819   AMOUNT OF BOND: $500
SECURITY: Jesse Atkins

LOOSE BONDS, page 65

ORPHAN: Burr, & Maurice H. Garland
PARENT: Rice Garland   GUARDIAN: Samuel Garland
DATE: 5 July 1819   AMOUNT OF BOND: $20,000
SECURITY: William Garland
          James Garland

. . . .

ORPHAN: Nicholas A. Garland
PARENT: Rice Garland   GUARDIAN: James Garland
DATE: 5 July 1819   AMOUNT OF BOND: $10,000
SECURITY: William Garland
          Samuel Garland

. . . .

ORPHAN: Reuben H. Martin
PARENT: Elisha Martin   GUARDIAN: Allen Foster
DATE: 3 Aug. 1819   AMOUNT OF BOND: $500
SECURITY: Meredith Kimbrough

. . . .

ORPHAN: Peggy E. Marr
PARENT: John Marr   GUARDIAN: Wilson Roberts
DATE: 6 Sept. 1819   AMOUNT OF BOND: $5,000
SECURITY: John Jones

. . . .

ORPHAN: Jacob Moon
PARENT: Richard Moon   GUARDIAN: Fleming B. Moon
DATE: 6 Sept. 1819   AMOUNT OF BOND: $1,500
SECURITY: Jeremiah Cleveland

LOOSE BONDS, page 66

ORPHAN: Samuel W. Moon
PARENT: Richard Moon   GUARDIAN: Richard Moore
DATE: 6 Sept. 1819   AMOUNT OF BOND: $1,500
SECURITY: Jeremiah Cleveland

. . . .

ORPHAN: Ann Townley
PARENT: Mann Townley   GUARDIAN: Nimrod Bramham
        [not deceased]
DATE: 4 Oct. 1819   AMOUNT OF BOND: $2,500
SECURITY: Buckner Townley

. . . .

ORPHAN: Barrett Dickenson
PARENT: John Dickenson   GUARDIAN: James Dowell
DATE: 2 Nov. 1819   AMOUNT OF BOND: $4,000
SECURITY: Thomas Wood
          Douglass Dickenson

. . . .

ORPHAN: Julius W., John N., William L., & Arramintha Clarkson
PARENT: Reuben Clarkson   GUARDIAN: [father] Reuben Clarkso[n]
DATE: 4 Nov. 1819   AMOUNT OF BOND: $6,000
SECURITY: James Clarkson

. . . .

ORPHAN: Ann Burnley
PARENT: John Burnley   GUARDIAN: Nathaniel Burnley
DATE: 6 Dec. 1819   AMOUNT OF BOND: $1,000
SECURITY: Seth Burnley

LOOSE BONDS, page 67

ORPHAN: Leah Eversole
PARENT: Abraham Eversole GUARDIAN: Spicer Humphrey
DATE: 6 Dec. 1819 AMOUNT OF BOND: $200
SECURITY: Richard Humphrey

. . . .

ORPHAN: Crenshaw Fretwell
PARENT: William Fretwell, Jr. GUARDIAN: Jemima Fretwell
DATE: 6 Dec. 1819 AMOUNT OF BOND: $500
SECURITY: Nicholas Burnley

. . . .

ORPHAN: Elizabeth Burrus
PARENT: Charles Burrus GUARDIAN: Edmund Davis
DATE: 4 Jan. 1820 AMOUNT OF BOND: $2,000
SECURITY: Dickenson Burrus

. . . .

ORPHAN: Joshua W. Abell
PARENT: Caleb Abell GUARDIAN: John S. Abell
DATE: 7 Feb. 1820 AMOUNT OF BOND: $6,000
SECURITY: Caleb S. Abell
          Benjamin Ficklen

. . . .

ORPHAN: Sarah Garner
PARENT: William G. Garner GUARDIAN: Mary Garner
DATE: 7 Feb. 1820[?] AMOUNT OF BOND: $50
SECURITY: Henry Chiles

LOOSE BONDS, page 68

ORPHAN: Polly Smith

PARENT: William Smith GUARDIAN: John Douglass

DATE: 7 Feb. 1820 AMOUNT OF BOND: $20,000

SECURITY: Thomas Edwards, Edward Fearneyhough, James Dowell

. . . .

ORPHAN: William, & Jane Maxwell

PARENT: Bezaleel Maxwell GUARDIAN: Samuel L. Hart

DATE: 6 March 1820 AMOUNT OF BOND: $1,000

SECURITY: Andrew Hart

. . . .

ORPHAN: Mary C. Barkley

PARENT: Robert Barkley GUARDIAN: William Moon

DATE: 7 March 1820 AMOUNT OF BOND: $6,000

SECURITY: John Harris

. . . .

ORPHAN: Mildred White

PARENT: Chapman White GUARDIAN: Chapman W. Maupin

DATE: 4 April 1820 AMOUNT OF BOND: $500

SECURITY: Brightberry Brown

. . . .

ORPHAN: Meed Carr

PARENT: Micajah Carr GUARDIAN: Barnett Carr

DATE: 1 May 1820 AMOUNT OF BOND: $1,000

SECURITY: Mekins Carr

LOOSE BONDS, page 69

ORPHAN: Sarah Ann Hays
PARENT: James Hays **GUARDIAN:** Robert Brooks
DATE: 1 May 1820 **AMOUNT OF BOND:** $5,000
SECURITY: John Hays

. . . .

ORPHAN: Harriet Gray
PARENT: William Gray **GUARDIAN:** Arthur S. Brockenbrough
DATE: 7 Aug. 1820 **AMOUNT OF BOND:** $6,000
SECURITY: John M. Perry

. . . .

ORPHAN: Elizabeth Casney
PARENT: Christopher Carsney **GUARDIAN:** George Eades
DATE: 9 Aug. 1820 **AMOUNT OF BOND:** $100
SECURITY: Tarlton Woodson

. . . .

ORPHAN: Mary McDaniel
PARENT: an illegitimate child of Sally McDaniel **GUARDIAN:** Benjamin Taylor
DATE: 4 Sept. 1820 **AMOUNT OF BOND:** $100
SECURITY: Peter Garland

. . . .

ORPHAN: James D. Allen
PARENT: Richard H. Allen **GUARDIAN:** Dabney Minor
DATE: 6 Nov. 1820 **AMOUNT OF BOND:** $15,000
SECURITY: Micajah Woods

LOOSE BONDS, page 70

ORPHAN:	Sarah Black		
PARENT:	Jacob Black	GUARDIAN:	John Bailey
DATE:	6 Nov. 1820	AMOUNT OF BOND:	$500
SECURITY:	Alexander Garrett		

. . . .

ORPHAN:	Ann B. Mullins		
PARENT:	John Mullins	GUARDIAN:	Ira B. Brown
DATE:	4 Dec. 1820	AMOUNT OF BOND:	$2,000
SECURITY:	James Jarman		

. . . .

ORPHAN:	Elizabeth Ann Clarkson [over 14 years of age]		
PARENT:	Julius Clarkson	GUARDIAN:	Jesse Lewis
DATE:	1 Jan. 1821	AMOUNT OF BOND:	$2,000
SECURITY:	Reuben Maury		

Note asks that grandfather, Jesse Lewis, be reappointed her guardian.

. . . .

ORPHAN:	Lindsay Martin		
PARENT:	Benjamin Martin	GUARDIAN:	Caleb S. Abell
DATE:	1 Jan. 1821	AMOUNT OF BOND:	$4,000
SECURITY:	Peter Garland		

. . . .

ORPHAN:	William Camp		
PARENT:	Ambrose Camp	GUARDIAN:	Laurence T. Catlett
DATE:	6 March 1821	AMOUNT OF BOND:	$500
SECURITY:	William Watson		

LOOSE BONDS, page 71

ORPHAN: William Maxwell
PARENT: Bezaleel Maxwell   GUARDIAN: Parsons Clarke
DATE: 7 May 1821   AMOUNT OF BOND: $600
SECURITY: James Norvell

. . . .

ORPHAN: Catharine Thomason
PARENT: Rice[?] Thomason   GUARDIAN: William F. Carden
DATE: 4 June 1821   AMOUNT OF BOND: $100
SECURITY: William Gamble

. . . .

ORPHAN: Elly Thacker
PARENT: Jesse Thacker   GUARDIAN: John Gay
DATE: 5 June 1821   AMOUNT OF BOND: $100
SECURITY: Phillip Phillips

. . . .

ORPHAN: Lucy Day
PARENT: [none given]   GUARDIAN: Thomas Beddow
DATE: 6 Aug. 1821   AMOUNT OF BOND: $100
SECURITY: Anthony P. Wilkerson

. . . .

ORPHAN: Darkey McCord
PARENT: William McCord   GUARDIAN: William Taylor
DATE: 6 Aug. 1821   AMOUNT OF BOND: $100
SECURITY: John Crank

LOOSE BONDS, page 72

ORPHAN: Cynthia, & Harriet Jopling
PARENT: Ralph Jopling   GUARDIAN: William Elsom
DATE: 6 Nov. 1821   AMOUNT OF BOND: $5,000
SECURITY: John Hall

. . . .

ORPHAN: Susan Hamner
PARENT: John Hamner   GUARDIAN: John B. Carr
        [not deceased]
DATE: 7 Nov. 1821   AMOUNT OF BOND: $1,000
SECURITY: David Gentry
          Dabney Carr

. . . .

ORPHAN: Jane Pleasants
PARENT: Sarah Bladden   GUARDIAN: David Spradling
DATE: 7 Nov. 1821   AMOUNT OF BOND: $50
SECURITY: Benjamin Essex

. . . .

ORPHAN: Henry, Durrett, Walker, Milly, Cally[?], & Ann Austin
PARENT: Henry Austin   GUARDIAN: David Austin
DATE: 3 Dec. 1821   AMOUNT OF BOND: $2,500
SECURITY: Garrett Austin, Thomas Austin, Ira B. Brown

. . . .

ORPHAN: Lucinda Becks
PARENT: Thomas Becks   GUARDIAN: Richard Sneed
DATE: 3 Dec. 1821   AMOUNT OF BOND: $100
SECURITY: Lucy Becks

LOOSE BONDS, page 73

ORPHAN: Levina Garrison
PARENT: John Garrison GUARDIAN: Matthew Turner
DATE: 3 Dec. 1821 AMOUNT OF BOND: $200
SECURITY: John Faris

. . . .

ORPHAN: Polly, & Betsy Maupin
PARENT: David Maupin GUARDIAN: John Maupin
DATE: 3 Dec. 1821 AMOUNT OF BOND: $2,500
SECURITY: Thomas Maupin

. . . .

ORPHAN: Jane Wills
PARENT: Thomas Wills GUARDIAN: William Watson
DATE: 3 Dec. 1821 AMOUNT OF BOND: $2,000
SECURITY: Samuel C. Barksdale

. . . .

ORPHAN: Rebecca Gray [over 14 years of age]
PARENT: William Gray GUARDIAN: Arthur A. Brockenbrou
DATE: 7 Jan. 1822 AMOUNT OF BOND: $8,000
SECURITY: Francis B. Dyer

. . . .

ORPHAN: James Mars
PARENT: John Mars GUARDIAN: John Jones
DATE: 4 Feb. 1822 AMOUNT OF BOND: $1,000
SECURITY: Benjamin Ficklen

LOOSE BONDS, page 74

ORPHAN: Martha, & Mary B. Anderson
PARENT: William Anderson GUARDIAN: John Gilmer
DATE: 4 March 1822 AMOUNT OF BOND: $6,000
SECURITY: Overton C. Anderson

. . . .

ORPHAN: Elizabeth Moore
PARENT: William Moore GUARDIAN: Wilson Bailey
DATE: 5 March 1822 AMOUNT OF BOND: $500
SECURITY: Michael Johnson

. . . .

ORPHAN: Henry W. Richardson
PARENT: Samuel Richardson GUARDIAN: Elijah Brown
DATE: 5 March 1822 AMOUNT OF BOND: $1,500
SECURITY: Benjamin Haden

. . . .

ORPHAN: Thomas J., & George W. Old
PARENT: John Old GUARDIAN: Robert Garland
DATE: 6 May 1822 AMOUNT OF BOND: $1,000
SECURITY: William Garland

. . . .

ORPHAN: George W. Gibson
        an illegitimate child
PARENT: [none given] GUARDIAN: William Stewardson
DATE: 1 July 1822 AMOUNT OF BOND: $500
SECURITY: George M. Woods

LOOSE BONDS, page 75

ORPHAN:	Chapman, & Fontaine Maupin		
PARENT:	Thomas Maupin	GUARDIAN:	[father] Thomas Maupin
DATE:	5 Aug. 1822	AMOUNT OF BOND:	$1,000
SECURITY:	Nathaniel Thompson		

. . . .

ORPHAN:	Mary Ann Garrison		
PARENT:	John Garrison	GUARDIAN:	Menoah Via
DATE:	7 Oct. 1822	AMOUNT OF BOND:	$100
SECURITY:	Mathew Turner		

. . . .

ORPHAN:	Martha W. Terrell		
PARENT:	William Terrell	GUARDIAN:	Daniel F. Carr
DATE:	7 Oct. 1822	AMOUNT OF BOND:	$3,000
SECURITY:	James O. Carr		

. . . .

ORPHAN:	Mary Wells		
PARENT:	Thomas Wells	GUARDIAN:	John C. Wells
DATE:	7 Oct. 1822	AMOUNT OF BOND:	$2,000
SECURITY:	Robert Brooks		

. . . .

ORPHAN:	Jane Maxwell		
PARENT:	Bezaleel Maxwell	GUARDIAN:	Parsons Clarke
DATE:	4 Nov. 1822	AMOUNT OF BOND:	$600
SECURITY:	James Norvell		

LOOSE BONDS, page 76

ORPHAN: Nicholas Thomas

PARENT: Charles L. Thomas GUARDIAN: John L. Thomas

DATE: 4 Nov. 1822 AMOUNT OF BOND: $6,000

SECURITY: John R. Jones, Nimrod Bramham, Opie Norris, John M. Perry

. . . .

ORPHAN: Alice Lewis

PARENT: Thomas W. Lewis GUARDIAN: James Clarke

DATE: 5 Nov. 1822 AMOUNT OF BOND: $5,000

SECURITY: John Fagg
Nicholas Lewis

. . . .

ORPHAN: Mary P., Eliza M., Emily A., Martha W., Thomas T., & Isaetta J. Eubank

PARENT: John Eubank GUARDIAN: Winifred Eubank

DATE: 3 Feb. 1823 AMOUNT OF BOND: $3,000

SECURITY: Wilson Eubank, George Eubank, Jacob Norris, James O. Walters

. . . .

ORPHAN: Patsy Luck

PARENT: Overton Luck GUARDIAN: Ephraim Wood

DATE: 3 Feb. 1823 AMOUNT OF BOND: $500

SECURITY: John Dickenson
Brice Edwards

. . . .

ORPHAN: Malinda Hays

PARENT: James Hays GUARDIAN: Robert Brooks

DATE: 3 March 1823 AMOUNT OF BOND: 1,000 pounds

SECURITY: John C. Wells
Benjamin Wheeler

LOOSE BONDS, page 77

ORPHAN: Jacob Grass
PARENT: John Grass   GUARDIAN: George W. Oliver
DATE: 5 May 1823   AMOUNT OF BOND: $1,500
SECURITY: Leonadas Holeman
          John Hill

. . . .

ORPHAN: Caroline Martin
PARENT: Benjamin Martin   GUARDIAN: Caleb S. Abell
DATE: 1 Sept. 1823   AMOUNT OF BOND: $1,200
SECURITY: George M[?] Woods

. . . .

ORPHAN: Charles Thomas
PARENT: Charles L. Thomas   GUARDIAN: John M. Martin
DATE: 7 Oct. 1823   AMOUNT OF BOND: $12,000
SECURITY: John L. Thomas
          Alexander Garrett

. . . .

ORPHAN: Martha Yancey
PARENT: Jechonias Yancey   GUARDIAN: Joel Yancey
DATE: 7 Oct. 1823   AMOUNT OF BOND: $100
SECURITY: Francis B. Dyer

. . . .

ORPHAN: Rixin Marr
PARENT: Thomas Marr   GUARDIAN: Gabriel Maupin
DATE: 3 Nov. 1823   AMOUNT OF BOND: $500
SECURITY: Henry Marr

LOOSE BONDS, page 78

ORPHAN: Pemily Marr
PARENT: Thomas Marr GUARDIAN: Henry Marr
DATE: 3 Nov. 1823 AMOUNT OF BOND: $500
SECURITY: Gabriel Maupin

. . . .

ORPHAN: Mary Ann Sarah Maupin
PARENT: Gabriel Maupin GUARDIAN: Gabriel Maupin
DATE: 3 Nov. 1823 AMOUNT OF BOND: $500
SECURITY: James D. Allen

. . . .

ORPHAN: Jane, & Robert Lewis
PARENT: Thomas W. Lewis GUARDIAN: Nicholas H. Lewis
DATE: 5 Nov. 1822 AMOUNT OF BOND: $10,000
SECURITY: James Leitch

. . . .

ORPHAN: John Martin
PARENT: Benjamin Martin GUARDIAN: Augustine Woodson
DATE: 1 Dec. 1823 AMOUNT OF BOND: $1,200
SECURITY: Joshua W. Abell

. . . .

ORPHAN: Austin Ballard
PARENT: Wilson Ballard GUARDIAN: David Austin
DATE: 5 Jan. 1824 AMOUNT OF BOND: $500
SECURITY: Thomas Austin

LOOSE BONDS, page 79

ORPHAN: Reuben Bishop
PARENT: Barbara Bishop GUARDIAN: William Hogg
DATE: 2 Feb. 1824 AMOUNT OF BOND: $100
SECURITY: Charles C. Lacy

. . . .

ORPHAN: Sarah R. Marrs
PARENT: John Marrs GUARDIAN: Wilson Roberts
DATE: 2 Feb. 1824 AMOUNT OF BOND: $500
SECURITY: William Harper

. . . .

ORPHAN: Robert W. Thomas
PARENT: Charles L. Thomas GUARDIAN: Valentine W. Southall
DATE: 2 March 1824 AMOUNT OF BOND: $4,000
SECURITY: John Winn
John L. Thomas

. . . .

ORPHAN: Frances Thomas
PARENT: Charles L. Thomas GUARDIAN: John M. Martin
DATE: 7 June 1824 AMOUNT OF BOND: $10,000
SECURITY: James Leitch
Nicholas L. Martin

. . . .

ORPHAN: Emeline, Maria, & Mary Jane Lewis
PARENT: John W. Lewis GUARDIAN: Howell Lewis
DATE: 9 June 1824 AMOUNT OF BOND: $1,000
SECURITY: John W. Thomas

LOOSE BONDS, page 80

ORPHAN: Frances C., & David Hutchens
PARENT: David Hutchens GUARDIAN: John Pilson
DATE: 2 Aug. 1824 AMOUNT OF BOND: $500
SECURITY: James Gillum

. . . .

ORPHAN: John Thomas
PARENT: Charles L. Thomas GUARDIAN: John L. Thomas
DATE: 5 Aug. 1824 AMOUNT OF BOND: $10,000
SECURITY: John M. Martin,
William C. Rives, V. W. Southall

. . . .

ORPHAN: Thomas Moon
"a legitimate child of"
PARENT: William Hopkins GUARDIAN: Larken Hudson
[not deceased]
DATE: 6 Sept. 1824 AMOUNT OF BOND: $100
SECURITY: Joseph Wingfield

. . . .

ORPHAN: Elizabeth Hamner
PARENT: William Hamner GUARDIAN: Robert Foster
DATE: 1 Nov. 1824 AMOUNT OF BOND: $100
SECURITY: Joshua Foster

. . . .

ORPHAN: Sarah McCord
PARENT: William McCord GUARDIAN: William Taylor
DATE: 1 Nov. 1824 AMOUNT OF BOND: $100
SECURITY: John Crank

LOOSE BONDS, page 81

ORPHAN: Sarah T. Anderson
PARENT: Edmund Anderson   GUARDIAN: Thomas F. Lewis
DATE: 6 Dec. 1824   AMOUNT OF BOND: $1,200
SECURITY: Howell Lewis

. . . .

ORPHAN: William W., & Mildred Minor
PARENT: Dabney Minor   GUARDIAN: Peter Minor
DATE: 6 Dec. 1824   AMOUNT OF BOND: $8,000
SECURITY: John Gilmer
          Alexander Garrett

. . . .

ORPHAN: Catharine, & Sarah Minor
PARENT: Dabney Minor   GUARDIAN: John Gilmer
DATE: 6 Dec. 1824   AMOUNT OF BOND: $8,000
SECURITY: Peter Minor
          Alexander Garrett

. . . .

ORPHAN: Mary L., Elizabeth A., Robert J., & Dorothy Mooreman
PARENT: Robert Mooreman   GUARDIAN: John T. Holman
DATE: 6 Dec. 1824   AMOUNT OF BOND: $10,000
SECURITY: John W. Argyle,
Samuel Childres, Overton Anderson

. . . .

ORPHAN: Joseph Rogers
PARENT: Achilles Rogers   GUARDIAN: John Rogers
DATE: 6 Dec. 1824   AMOUNT OF BOND: $600
SECURITY: Edmund Davis

SECTION II

BOND BOOK

1829 - 1844

II, pages 1 thru 9

ORPHAN: Lucinda Blain
PARENT: Alexander Blain   GUARDIAN: William D. Hart
DATE: 4 March 1829   AMOUNT OF BOND: $2,000
SECURITY: James M. Payne   PAGE: 1

. . . .

ORPHAN: James A. McAllester
PARENT: James McAllester   GUARDIAN: Thomas Lane
DATE: 6 March 1829   AMOUNT OF BOND: $700
SECURITY: William Tullock   PAGE: 3

. . . .

ORPHAN: John O., & Andrew H. Young
PARENT: David Young   GUARDIAN: William D. Hart
DATE: 2 March 1829   AMOUNT OF BOND: $2,000
SECURITY: James Hart   PAGE: 5

. . . .

ORPHAN: Emeline, Elmira, Samuel H., & Lucian Young
PARENT: David Young   GUARDIAN: William D. Hart
DATE: 2 March 1829   AMOUNT OF BOND: $400
SECURITY: James Hart   PAGE: 7

. . . .

ORPHAN: Sarah A. Campbell
PARENT: John R. Campbell   GUARDIAN: [father] John R. Campbell
DATE: 4 May 1829   AMOUNT OF BOND: $2,000
SECURITY: John Watson   PAGE: 9
Note states that she has been left a legacy by William McKapon of Pennsylvania.

II, pages 11 thru 19

ORPHAN: Mildred A. Marshall
PARENT: James Marshall   GUARDIAN: Benjamin Robinson
DATE: 4 May 1829   AMOUNT OF BOND: $200
SECURITY: William Brockman   PAGE: 11

. . . .

ORPHAN: Eliza Allfred
PARENT: James Allfred   GUARDIAN: Tandy Sprouse
DATE: 1 June 1829   AMOUNT OF BOND: $25
SECURITY: John B. Spiece   PAGE: 13

. . . .

ORPHAN: Dorithy Crenshaw
PARENT: William Crenshaw   GUARDIAN: David Thompson
DATE: 6 July 1829   AMOUNT OF BOND: $5,000
SECURITY: John D. Foster   PAGE: 15

. . . .

ORPHAN: Catharine M. Spencer
PARENT: Charles Spencer   GUARDIAN: Jefferson Clark
DATE: 6 July 1829   AMOUNT OF BOND: $2,000
SECURITY: Frank Carr   PAGE: 17
Note on page 40 states that Catharine M. Spencer was the daughter of Charles (who died 16 Mar. 1829) and Elizabeth Wray Spencer.

. . . .

ORPHAN: William B., & Mildred B. Watts [over 14 years of age],
          Nathan, & Nancy Watts
PARENT: Phillip Watts   GUARDIAN: [brother] John B. Wat
DATE: 6 July 1829   AMOUNT OF BOND: $5,400
SECURITY: Joseph Alexander,   PAGE: 19
George W. Kinsolving, Nelson Barksdale

II, pages 21 thru 29

ORPHAN: Mary Barnett
PARENT: Judy Barnett GUARDIAN: Garrett Tyree
DATE: 3 Aug. 1829 AMOUNT OF BOND: $200
SECURITY: James B. Rogers PAGE: 21

. . . .

ORPHAN: Mary Carter Wood
PARENT: John H. Wood GUARDIAN: Elizabeth W. Spencer
DATE: 4 Aug. 1829 AMOUNT OF BOND: $1,600
SECURITY: Richard Duke PAGE: 23

. . . .

ORPHAN: John Taylor
PARENT: Susan Taylor
[not deceased] GUARDIAN: Rice W. Wood
DATE: 8 Sept. 1829 AMOUNT OF BOND: $10
SECURITY: Ira Garrett PAGE: 25

. . . .

ORPHAN: Sarah Ann Cromwell
PARENT: Jesse Cromwell GUARDIAN: Thomas Fadley
DATE: 5 Oct. 1829 AMOUNT OF BOND: $100
SECURITY: John M. Perry PAGE: 27

. . . .

ORPHAN: Parmelia E. Gentry
PARENT: David Gentry GUARDIAN: Charles W. Hanner
DATE: 5 Oct. 1829 AMOUNT OF BOND: $1,500
SECURITY: John Dunkum PAGE: 29
Thomas Ammonet

II, pages 31 thru 39

ORPHAN: Mary Rippeto
PARENT: Peter Rippeto GUARDIAN: Ephraim Bowen
DATE: 5 Oct. 1829 AMOUNT OF BOND: $100
SECURITY: Benjamin Moore PAGE: 31

. . . .

ORPHAN: Amanda W. Kinsolving
PARENT: James Kinsolving GUARDIAN: George W. Kinsolving
DATE: 2 Nov. 1829 AMOUNT OF BOND: $3,000
SECURITY: Thomas Maupin PAGE: 33
Jefferson B. Kinsolving

. . . .

ORPHAN: Napoleon B. L. Kinsolving
PARENT: James Kinsolving GUARDIAN: Jefferson B. Kinsolving
DATE: 2 Nov. 1829 AMOUNT OF BOND: $3,000
SECURITY: Henry White, PAGE: 35
George W. Kinsolving, Madison B. G. Kinsolving

. . . .

ORPHAN: Mary Martin
PARENT: Samuel Martin GUARDIAN: Reuben Coles
DATE: 2 Nov. 1829 AMOUNT OF BOND: $25
SECURITY: Allerson Butler PAGE: 37

. . . .

ORPHAN: Benjamin Martin
PARENT: Benjamin Martin GUARDIAN: Caleb S. Abell
DATE: 2 Nov. 1829 AMOUNT OF BOND: $1,400
SECURITY: John Martin PAGE: 39
Henry White

II, pages 41 thru 49

ORPHAN:	Martha M., Julia, & Charles Spencer		
PARENT:	Charles Spencer	GUARDIAN:	Elizabeth Spencer
DATE:	3 Nov. 1829	AMOUNT OF BOND:	$1,500
SECURITY:	Richard Duke	PAGE:	41

. . . .

ORPHAN:	Mary Proctor		
PARENT:	Joseph B. Proctor	GUARDIAN:	Sydner R. Pettitt
DATE:	7 Dec. 1829	AMOUNT OF BOND:	$500
SECURITY:	John Harvard	PAGE:	43

. . . .

ORPHAN:	Louisa Ure		
PARENT:	[left blank] Ure	GUARDIAN:	Hardin Massie
DATE:	7 Dec. 1829	AMOUNT OF BOND:	$100
SECURITY:	Ira Garrett	PAGE:	45

. . . .

ORPHAN:	Rufus K. Dawson		
PARENT:	Allen Dawson	GUARDIAN:	William W. Dawson
DATE:	4 Jan. 1830	AMOUNT OF BOND:	$100
SECURITY:	Daniel M. Railey	PAGE:	47

. . . .

ORPHAN:	Martin A. Dawson		
PARENT:	Allen Dawson	GUARDIAN:	Frank Carr
DATE:	4 Jan. 1830	AMOUNT OF BOND:	$100
SECURITY:	W. H. Meriwether	PAGE:	49

II, pages 51 thru 59

ORPHAN: Jane Salmon
PARENT: Thomas Salmon	GUARDIAN: James Early
DATE: 4 Jan. 1830	AMOUNT OF BOND: $1,500
SECURITY: William Early	PAGE: 51

. . . .

ORPHAN: Martha Salmon
PARENT: Thomas Salmon	GUARDIAN: James Early
DATE: 4 Jan. 1830	AMOUNT OF BOND: $1,500
SECURITY: William Early	PAGE: 53

. . . .

ORPHAN: Lucy Jane Bernard
PARENT: Joseph Bernard	GUARDIAN: William D. Fitch
DATE: 3 May 1830	AMOUNT OF BOND: $100
SECURITY: Harden Massie	PAGE: 55

. . . .

ORPHAN: Mary Esken
PARENT: John Esken	GUARDIAN: Samuel Falwell
DATE: 3 May 1830	AMOUNT OF BOND: $50
SECURITY: Benjamin Farish	PAGE: 57

. . . .

ORPHAN: Henry Thacker
PARENT: Ezekiel Thacker	GUARDIAN: [father] Ezekial Thack
DATE: 10 June 1830	AMOUNT OF BOND: $40
SECURITY: Randal Sprouce,	PAGE: 59
Benjamin Thacker, Polly Grimes,
Benjamin Moore

II, pages 61 thru 69

ORPHAN: Frances, John, Rebecca, Elizabeth, & Martha Gilmore
PARENT: William Gilmore   GUARDIAN: John Gilmore
DATE: 2 Aug. 1830   AMOUNT OF BOND: $6,000
SECURITY: John T. Holman   PAGE: 61
          John H. Coleman

. . . .

ORPHAN: Susan Thacker
PARENT: Betsey Thacker   GUARDIAN: James Hurt
        [not deceased?]
DATE: 6 Sept. 1830   AMOUNT OF BOND: $25
SECURITY: John B. Spiece   PAGE: 63

. . . .

ORPHAN: Andrew J. Humphrey
PARENT: Isaiah Humphrey   GUARDIAN: George W. Kinsolving
DATE: 6 Sept. 1830   AMOUNT OF BOND: $300
SECURITY: Thomas W. Gooch   PAGE: 65

. . . .

ORPHAN: James, Washington P., Mary Ann, & John M. Lobban
PARENT: James Lobban   GUARDIAN: [father] James Lobban
DATE: 6 Sept. 1830   AMOUNT OF BOND: $2,000
SECURITY: John Lobban   PAGE: 67

. . . .

ORPHAN: George C., John H., Maria J., Ann H., Martha J., & Lucy W. Gilmer
PARENT: Thomas W. Gilmer   GUARDIAN: Thomas W. Gilmer
DATE: 6 Sept. 1830   AMOUNT OF BOND: $30,000
SECURITY: John Gilmer   PAGE: 69
John A. G. Davis, Rice W. Wood

Note on page 68, signed by Maria J. Gilmer, asks that her brother Thomas W. Gilmer be appointed her guardian.

II, pages 71 thru 79

ORPHAN: Anne Anderson

PARENT: Frances Anderson [not deceased?]   GUARDIAN: James Hurt

DATE: 6 Sept. 1830   AMOUNT OF BOND: $25

SECURITY: John B. Spiece   PAGE: 71

• •

ORPHAN: Catharine Anderson

PARENT: James Anderson   GUARDIAN: Randolph Gypson

DATE: 3 Jan. 1831   AMOUNT OF BOND: $25

SECURITY: John B. Spiece   PAGE: 73

• •

ORPHAN: Sarah Farrar

PARENT: Joseph Farrar   GUARDIAN: John T. Holman

DATE: 3 Jan. 1831   AMOUNT OF BOND: $3,000

SECURITY: John Gantt, John Morris, Samuel Childres   PAGE: 75

• •

ORPHAN: John F. Weidemyer

PARENT: John M. Weidemyer   GUARDIAN: Thomas Draffen

DATE: 3 Jan. 1831   AMOUNT OF BOND: $30

SECURITY: Ira Harris   PAGE: 77

• •

ORPHAN: Richard Durrett

PARENT: James Durrett   GUARDIAN: Garrett White

DATE: 7 Feb. 1831   AMOUNT OF BOND: $4,000

SECURITY: John White   PAGE: 79

II, pages 81 thru 89

ORPHAN: Emily Martin
PARENT: Benjamin Martin   GUARDIAN: Richard S. Abell
DATE: 7 Feb. 1831   AMOUNT OF BOND: $4,000
SECURITY: John S. Abell   PAGE: 81

• •

ORPHAN: Rebecca Thurmond
PARENT: William Thurmond   GUARDIAN: Benjamin Thurmond
DATE: 7 March 1831   AMOUNT OF BOND: $600
SECURITY: William M. Thurmond   PAGE: 83

• •

ORPHAN: Sarah Drumheller
PARENT: Jacob Drumheller   GUARDIAN: Tarlton Woodson, Jr.
DATE: 4 April 1831   AMOUNT OF BOND: $500
SECURITY: John Davis   PAGE: 85

• •

ORPHAN: Mary Jane Noel
PARENT: Thompson Noel   GUARDIAN: George A. Scruggs
DATE: 2 May 1831   AMOUNT OF BOND: $150
SECURITY: Peter White   PAGE: 87

• •

ORPHAN: James, & Frances Michie
PARENT: William Michie   GUARDIAN: James Michie
DATE: 6 June 1831   AMOUNT OF BOND: $6,000
SECURITY: George Crank   PAGE: 89
Edmund Davis

II, pages 91 thru 101

ORPHAN:	Martha P. Moon
PARENT: Littleberry Moon	GUARDIAN: Littleberry Moon
DATE: 1 Aug. 1831	AMOUNT OF BOND: $6,000
SECURITY: Samuel O. Moon	PAGE: 91

. . . .

ORPHAN:	Warren Woodson
PARENT: Stephen Woodson	GUARDIAN: Overton C. Anderson
DATE: 3 Aug. 1831	AMOUNT OF BOND: $1,000
SECURITY: Benjamin M. Perkins Thomas W. Gilmer	PAGE: 93

. . . .

ORPHAN:	Agness Keaton
PARENT: Nelson Keaton	GUARDIAN: Charles Burrus
DATE: 5 Sept. 1831	AMOUNT OF BOND: $100
SECURITY: Nicholas Maupin	PAGE: 95

. . . . [page 97 was blank] . . . .

ORPHAN:	James, & Goodridge Garland
PARENT: Peter Garland	GUARDIAN: Henry White
DATE: 7 Nov. 1831	AMOUNT OF BOND: $100
SECURITY: William Woods	PAGE: 99

. . . .

ORPHAN:	William Marshall Morris
PARENT: William Morris	GUARDIAN: Nancy D. Morris
DATE: 7 Nov. 1831	AMOUNT OF BOND: $20,000
SECURITY: Dabney Carr, Marcus Durrett, Henry C. Moore, Henry White	PAGE: 101

II, pages 103 thru 111

ORPHAN:	Virginia Spradling
	illegitimate child of
PARENT:	Virginia Spradling
GUARDIAN:	Henry Thacker
DATE:	7 Nov. 1831
AMOUNT OF BOND:	$50
SECURITY:	Ezekial Thacker
PAGE:	103

* *

ORPHAN: James, & Margaret Hopkins
PARENT: William Hopkins   GUARDIAN: William Haden
DATE: 2 Jan. 1832   AMOUNT OF BOND: $4,000
SECURITY: Peter Porter   PAGE: 105
          Henry Turner

* *

ORPHAN: Louisa Cooper
PARENT: George Cooper   GUARDIAN: Ebenezer Watts
DATE: 6 Feb. 1832   AMOUNT OF BOND: $600
SECURITY: Samuel Leitch   PAGE: 107

* *

ORPHAN: Elizabeth, & Catharine Noel
PARENT: Thompson Noel   GUARDIAN: George A. Scruggs
DATE: 5 March 1832   AMOUNT OF BOND: $500
SECURITY: John D. Moon   PAGE: 109

* *

ORPHAN: John J. Thomas
PARENT: Charles L. Thomas   GUARDIAN: Charles S. Thomas
DATE: 7 May 1832   AMOUNT OF BOND: $6,000
SECURITY: John L. Thomas   PAGE: 111
          Charles J. Merewether

II, pages 113 thru 121

ORPHAN:	Warren, Ann S., & Daniel Woodson		
PARENT:	Stephen Woodson	GUARDIAN:	Peter White
DATE:	6 Aug. 1832	AMOUNT OF BOND:	$10,000
SECURITY:	Overton C. Anderson	PAGE:	113

. . . .

ORPHAN:	Mary Elizabeth Woodson		
PARENT:	Stephen Woodson	GUARDIAN:	Overton C. Anderson
DATE:	6 Aug. 1832	AMOUNT OF BOND:	$10,000
SECURITY:	Peter White	PAGE:	115

. . . .

ORPHAN:	Elizabeth Mundy		
PARENT:	Joseph Fox	GUARDIAN:	Tipton Sprouce
DATE:	3 Dec. 1832	AMOUNT OF BOND:	$20
SECURITY:	George Sprouce	PAGE:	117

. . . .

ORPHAN:	Richard Montgomery Durrett		
PARENT:	Davis Durrett	GUARDIAN:	Thomas Durrett
DATE:	7 Jan. 1833	AMOUNT OF BOND:	$8,000
SECURITY:	James Early, Robert Durrett, Garland Garth	PAGE:	119

. . . .

ORPHAN:	Francis Wood		
PARENT:	Robert Wood	GUARDIAN:	William Wood
DATE:	7 Jan. 1833	AMOUNT OF BOND:	$1,000
SECURITY:	David Wood	PAGE:	121

ORPHAN: Jane Baily
PARENT: James Baily   GUARDIAN: Thomas W. Harris
DATE: 4 Feb. 1833   AMOUNT OF BOND: $250
SECURITY: Ira Harris   PAGE: 123

. . . .

ORPHAN: Charles L. Garrison
PARENT: John Garrison   GUARDIAN: Matthew Turner
DATE: 4 Feb. 1833   AMOUNT OF BOND: $40
SECURITY: Henry White   PAGE: 125

. . . .

ORPHAN: Lucy Martin
PARENT: Thomas Martin   GUARDIAN: William V. Garland
DATE: 4 Feb. 1833   AMOUNT OF BOND: $1,500
SECURITY: Henry White   PAGE: 127

. . . .

ORPHAN: Mary E., Martha C., Virginia Eliza Garth
PARENT: Brightberry B. Garth   GUARDIAN: [father] Brightberry B. Garth
DATE: 4 March 1833   AMOUNT OF BOND: $3,000
SECURITY: Jesse Garth   PAGE: 129

. . . .

ORPHAN: Nancy Scruggs
PARENT: Benjamin Scruggs   GUARDIAN: William Suddarth
DATE: 5 March 1833   AMOUNT OF BOND: $200
SECURITY: Benjamin Moore   PAGE: 131

II, pages 133 thru 141

ORPHAN: Charles Lewis Bankhead

PARENT: Charles L. Bankhead   GUARDIAN: Samuel H. Lewis

DATE: 2 Sept. 1833   AMOUNT OF BOND: $16,000

SECURITY: George Gilmer   PAGE: 133
          Jacob Strayer

On page 132, Mary Jane Bankhead of Port Republic, Rockingham Co., Va., widow of Charles L. Bankhead, renounces right of guardianship of her son, Charles Lewis Bankhead. She asks that her friend and kinsman, Samuel H. Lewis of Rockingham County, be appointed in her stead. She states that Charles L. Bankhead was late of Albemarle County. It is further stated that the two securities, George Gilmer and Jacob Strayer are also of Rockingham County.

. . . .

ORPHAN: John D., Elizabeth A., Mary M., Charlott D., Ann M., & Martha L. Moon

PARENT: Jacob Moon   GUARDIAN: William H. Johnston
        [not deceased]

DATE: 2 Sept. 1833   AMOUNT OF BOND: $12,000

SECURITY: John D. Craven,   PAGE: 137
William J. Michie, Benjamin H. Magruder

. . . .

ORPHAN: William S. Bankhead

PARENT: Charles L. Bankhead   GUARDIAN: John C. Carter

DATE: 7 Oct. 1833   AMOUNT OF BOND: $20,000

SECURITY: Robert Carter   PAGE: 139
          Charles Carter

. . . .

ORPHAN: Thomas M. R. Bankhead

PARENT: Charles L. Bankhead   GUARDIAN: William Bankhead
                                             [of Caroline Co., Va.]
DATE: 7 Oct. 1833   AMOUNT OF BOND: $20,000

SECURITY: John Bankhead   PAGE: 141

On page 140, John Bankhead, Sr., of Caroline County, states that he is the grandfather of Thomas M. R. Bankhead

II, pages 143 thru 151

ORPHAN: Elizabeth C., & John L. Martin
PARENT: Lindsay Martin GUARDIAN: Joshua W. Abell
DATE: 7 Nov. 1833 AMOUNT OF BOND: $2,400
SECURITY: John Woodson PAGE: 143
John Martin

. . . .

ORPHAN: Frances Early
PARENT: John Early GUARDIAN: Joab Early
DATE: 2 Dec. 1833 AMOUNT OF BOND: $4,000
SECURITY: James Chapman PAGE: 145

. . . .

ORPHAN: Joseph R. Early
PARENT: John Early GUARDIAN: James T. Early
DATE: 2 Dec. 1833 AMOUNT OF BOND: $4,000
SECURITY: Edward Fearnyhough PAGE: 147

. . . .

ORPHAN: Jeremiah, & William Early
PARENT: John Early GUARDIAN: Margaret Early
DATE: 2 Dec. 1833 AMOUNT OF BOND: $8,000
SECURITY: Nelson Barksdale PAGE: 149

. . . .

ORPHAN: Sarah Eliza, & John E. Fearneyhough
PARENT: Edward Fearneyhough GUARDIAN: [father] Edward Fearneyho
DATE: 2 Dec. 1833 AMOUNT OF BOND: $4,000
SECURITY: James T. Early PAGE: 151
Bond states that these are the children of "Edward Farneyhough and Elizabeth his wife late Elizabeth Early".

II, pages 153 thru 161

ORPHAN: Joseph Norris
PARENT: John Norris
GUARDIAN: Opie Norris
DATE: 6 Jan. 1834
AMOUNT OF BOND: $1,000
SECURITY: John Rothwell
PAGE: 153

. . . .

ORPHAN: Frances Burton
PARENT: William C. Burton
GUARDIAN: Addison Johnson
DATE: 3 Feb. 1834
AMOUNT OF BOND: $2,000
SECURITY: Joshua Johnson
Mary F. Burton
PAGE: 155

. . . .

ORPHAN: Ellen W. Pates [over 14 years of age]
PARENT: [left blank] Pates
GUARDIAN: John P. Halbach
DATE: 4 March 1834
AMOUNT OF BOND: $100
SECURITY: Lucian Minor
PAGE: 157

. . . .

ORPHAN: Nancy Thomas
PARENT: Jesse Thomas
GUARDIAN: John L. Thomas
DATE: 3 March 1834
AMOUNT OF BOND: $600
SECURITY: Robert Hall
John W. Mayo
PAGE: 159

. . . .

ORPHAN: James Garland
PARENT: Peter Garland
GUARDIAN: Caleb S. Abell
DATE: 2 June 1834
AMOUNT OF BOND: $2,000
SECURITY: John Martin,
Richard S. Abell, Henry White
PAGE: 161

II, pages 163 thru 171

ORPHAN: John Burgess
PARENT: Glenford Burgess   GUARDIAN: Martin True[?]
DATE: 7 July 1834   AMOUNT OF BOND: $100
SECURITY: Nicholas Gianniny   PAGE: 163

· ·

ORPHAN: Mary Ann, & William Piper
PARENT: William Piper   GUARDIAN: Elizabeth Piper
DATE: 7 July 1834   AMOUNT OF BOND: $2,800
SECURITY: Garrett White   PAGE: 165

· ·

ORPHAN: Francis Wayman
PARENT: John Wayman   GUARDIAN: John Simpson, Jr.
DATE: 8 July 1834   AMOUNT OF BOND: $100
SECURITY: Nimrod Bramham   PAGE: 167

· ·

ORPHAN: James & Albert McGehee
PARENT: Joseph McGehee   GUARDIAN: Mary L. McGehee
DATE: 4 Aug. 1834   AMOUNT OF BOND: $500
SECURITY: Joseph McGehee   PAGE: 169
          William McGehee

· ·

ORPHAN: Mary, & Charles McGehee
PARENT: Joseph McGehee   GUARDIAN: Mary L. McGehee
DATE: 4 Aug. 1834   AMOUNT OF BOND: $500
SECURITY: Joseph McGehee   PAGE: 171
          William McGehee

II, pages 173 thru 181

ORPHAN: William Young

PARENT: William Young [not deceased?] GUARDIAN: Joseph Bishop

DATE: 4 Aug. 1834 AMOUNT OF BOND: $100

SECURITY: Ezra M. Wolfe PAGE: 173

. . . .

ORPHAN: Susan F., Edward F., & Elizabeth W. Birckhead

PARENT: Thomas Birckhead GUARDIAN: Mildred Birckhead

DATE: 1 Sept. 1834 AMOUNT OF BOND: $18,000

SECURITY: Edward Fearneyhough PAGE: 175
Francis Birckhead

. . . .

ORPHAN: Sarah E. Rolls

PARENT: Charles Rolls GUARDIAN: John Dunkum

DATE: 1 Sept. 1834 AMOUNT OF BOND: $200

SECURITY: John S. Abell PAGE: 177

. . . .

ORPHAN: Ann J. Bowles

PARENT: Kitty Bowles GUARDIAN: John Dunkum

DATE: 6 Oct. 1834 AMOUNT OF BOND: $50

SECURITY: Francis B. Dyer PAGE: 179

. . . .

ORPHAN: Mildred, & William Beck

PARENT: Reuben Beck GUARDIAN: James Duke

DATE: 6 Oct. 1834 AMOUNT OF BOND: $1,000

SECURITY: Zachariah Shackelford PAGE: 181
Robert D. Durrett

II, pages 183 thru 191

ORPHAN: Reuben M. Beck
PARENT: Reuben Beck   GUARDIAN: Andrew Beck
DATE: 6 Oct. 1834   AMOUNT OF BOND: $500
SECURITY: James Howell Lewis PAGE: 183

. . . .

ORPHAN: Catharine B. Thompson
PARENT: David Thompson   GUARDIAN: Dorothy C. Thompson
DATE: 3 Nov. 1834   AMOUNT OF BOND: $2,000
SECURITY: Nathaniel Thompson, Jr. PAGE: 185

. . . .

ORPHAN: Thomas, Elizabeth, George, & James Travillian
PARENT: James Travillian   GUARDIAN: John Carr
DATE: 4 Nov. 1834   AMOUNT OF BOND: $1,000
SECURITY: George Carr   PAGE: 187

. . . .

ORPHAN: Nelson, & John Travillian
PARENT: James Travillian   GUARDIAN: John Carr
DATE: 4 Nov. 1834   AMOUNT OF BOND: $1,000
SECURITY: George Carr   PAGE: 189

. . . .

ORPHAN: Etta Mallory
PARENT: Thomas Mallory   GUARDIAN: Bushrod B. Chiles
DATE: 1 Dec. 1834   AMOUNT OF BOND: $100
SECURITY: Benjamin F. Trice PAGE: 191

II, pages 193 thru 201

ORPHAN: Sarah, Ambrose B., Nancy E., & Durrett M. Hill
PARENT: John Hill   GUARDIAN: Bezaleel Brown
DATE: 5 Jan. 1835   AMOUNT OF BOND: $4,000
SECURITY: William Brown PAGE: 193

. . . .

ORPHAN: Louisa Jane, Evelina B., Elizabeth F., & Lucy T. Pace
PARENT: Harry Pace   GUARDIAN: Joseph Bishop
DATE: 5 Jan. 1835   AMOUNT OF BOND: $4,000
SECURITY: John D. Craven,   PAGE: 195
William P. Farish, Isaac Marshall

. . . .

ORPHAN: Francis L., John T., Lilbourn M., Henry O., & Elizabeth E. Au
PARENT: Obediah Austin   GUARDIAN: Francis Birckhead
DATE: 2 Feb. 1835   AMOUNT OF BOND: $6,000
SECURITY: Richard W. Birckhead PAGE: 197
Francis Birckhead, Jr.

. . . .

ORPHAN: Thomas, James, & Robert Baber
PARENT: James Baber   GUARDIAN: Benjamin Thurmond
DATE: 2 Feb. 1835   AMOUNT OF BOND: $1,000
SECURITY: William M. Thurmond PAGE: 199

. . . .

ORPHAN: Catharine, & Maria Brand
PARENT: Chiles Brand   GUARDIAN: Thomas R. Bailey
        [not deceased]
DATE: 2 Feb. 1835   AMOUNT OF BOND: $1,000
SECURITY: Isaac Marshall PAGE: 201

ORPHAN: John, & Thomas Birckhead
PARENT: John Birckhead GUARDIAN: Richard W. Birckhead
DATE: 2 Feb. 1835 AMOUNT OF BOND: $12,000
SECURITY: [none] PAGE: 203

. . . .

ORPHAN: Dulcema Hays
PARENT: John Hays GUARDIAN: Rice Bailey
DATE: 2 Feb. 1835 AMOUNT OF BOND: $500
SECURITY: John Gates PAGE: 205

. . . .

ORPHAN: Margaret, & William Thombs
PARENT: Samuel Thombs GUARDIAN: [father] Samuel Thombs
DATE: 7 April 1835 AMOUNT OF BOND: $1,000
SECURITY: Thomas W. Gilmer PAGE: 207

. . . .

ORPHAN: Peter C. Minor
PARENT: Peter Minor GUARDIAN: George G. Minor
DATE: 1 June 1835 AMOUNT OF BOND: $12,000
SECURITY: Hugh Minor PAGE: 209

. . . .

ORPHAN: Jane E. Scott
PARENT: Robert Scott GUARDIAN: James R. Watson
DATE: 5 Aug. 1835 AMOUNT OF BOND: $1,000
SECURITY: Ira Garrett PAGE: 211

II, pages 213 thru 221

ORPHAN: James, & Reuben Thomas
PARENT: Hudson Thomas GUARDIAN: Ralph Thomas
DATE: 3 Aug. 1835 AMOUNT OF BOND: $800
SECURITY: John Morris PAGE: 213

• •

ORPHAN: Ann Elizabeth, & James H. Burnley
PARENT: Seth Burnley GUARDIAN: [father] Seth Burnley
DATE: 7 Sept. 1835 AMOUNT OF BOND: $1,000
SECURITY: Thomas H. Brown PAGE: 215

• •

ORPHAN: Susan Eliza Ann Durrett
PARENT: James Durrett GUARDIAN: [father] James Durrett
DATE: 7 Sept. 1835 AMOUNT OF BOND: $1,000
SECURITY: William Goodman PAGE: 217

• •

ORPHAN: Susan Eliza Ann Durrett
PARENT: James Durrett GUARDIAN: [father] James Durrett
DATE: 7 Dec. 1835 AMOUNT OF BOND: $1,500
SECURITY: William Goodman PAGE: 219

• •

ORPHAN: Richard L. Farrar
PARENT: John S. Farrar GUARDIAN: William J. Robertson
DATE: 4 Jan. 1836 AMOUNT OF BOND: $3,000
SECURITY: Jesse Jopling PAGE: 221
Nathaniel Goolsby

II, pages 223 thru 229

ORPHAN: Martha G., Lavenia M., Sophia J., & Marcellus Farrar

PARENT: John S. Farrar　　GUARDIAN: Sarah J. Farrar

DATE: 4 Jan. 1836　　AMOUNT OF BOND: $10,000

SECURITY: Jesse Jopling, John Crank, Nathaniel Goolsby　　PAGE: 223

   This bond is accompanied on page 223 by releases from guardianship to their mother, Mrs. Sarah J. Farrar, widow and relict of the late John S. Farrar, from her children: John S. Farrar, D. N. Jones, and Martha G. Farrar - dated 8 March 1849. Another letter of release dated 8 April 1844 is signed by Garrett W. Piper as husband of Sophia Farrar.

* *

ORPHAN: Mary J. Peake

PARENT: William Peake　　GUARDIAN: John Dunkum

DATE: 4 Jan. 1836　　AMOUNT OF BOND: $1,000

SECURITY: William Dunkum　　PAGE: 225

* *

ORPHAN: Strother Bruffy

PARENT: George Bruffy　　GUARDIAN: Benjamin Moore

DATE: 7 March 1836　　AMOUNT OF BOND: $25

SECURITY: James Hurt　　PAGE: 227

* *

ORPHAN: Charles R., Elizabeth A., Robert B., Mary J., Samuel M., John F., Celeste P. C. L., & Sarah F. A. W. Slaughter

PARENT: Robert Slaughter　　GUARDIAN: Mary R. Slaughter

DATE: 8 March 1836　　AMOUNT OF BOND: $4,000

SECURITY: Samuel Garland　　PAGE: 229

II, pages 231 thru 239

ORPHAN: Elizabeth D. Brown

PARENT: Bernard Brown GUARDIAN: Clifton Brown

DATE: 2 May 1836 AMOUNT OF BOND: $600

SECURITY: Dabney M. Jarman PAGE: 231

. . . .

ORPHAN: Richard A., Catharine N., Maria L., William W., Lucy E., James W., Sarah R., & Robert Brand

PARENT: Chiles Brand [not deceased] GUARDIAN: William J. Duke

DATE: 2 May 1836 AMOUNT OF BOND: $2,000

SECURITY: John J. Bowcock PAGE: 233

. . . .

ORPHAN: Mary Louisa Minor

PARENT: Peter Minor GUARDIAN: Franklin Minor

DATE: 2 May 1836 AMOUNT OF BOND: [left blank]

SECURITY: Hugh Minor PAGE: 235

. . . .

ORPHAN: John S. Minor

PARENT: Peter Minor GUARDIAN: Hugh Minor

DATE: 2 May 1836 AMOUNT OF BOND: [left blank]

SECURITY: Franklin Minor PAGE: 237

. . . .

ORPHAN: Mary Ann Shackleford

PARENT: James Shackleford GUARDIAN: Nathaniel Burnley

DATE: 2 May 1836 AMOUNT OF BOND: $300

SECURITY: Thomas Wood PAGE: 239

II, pages 241 thru 249

ORPHAN: Anne, Cornelia, Mary, & Antoinette Wood
PARENT: Rice W. Wood   GUARDIAN: Thomas Wood
DATE: 2 May 1836   AMOUNT OF BOND: $50,000
SECURITY: Drury Wood   PAGE: 241
          Nathaniel Burnley

On page 240 there is a note from Sarah Wood asking that Thomas Wood be appointed guardian to her daughters: Anne, Cornelia, Mary, & Antoinette. Ages are stated as follows: Anne, between 14 & 15; Cornelia, about 12; Mary, about 10; and Antoinette about 7 or 8. The whole estate is estimated to have a value of about $25,000, of which the widow is entitled to 1/3 during her life.

. . . .

ORPHAN: Julia, & Shelby Carr
PARENT: Overton W. Carr   GUARDIAN: Bernard Carr
DATE: 1 Aug. 1836   AMOUNT OF BOND: $2,500
SECURITY: James Eastham   PAGE: 243
          Rice Maupin

. . . .

ORPHAN: Thornton O., Julia A., Celia B., & John A. Rogers
PARENT: Thornton Rogers   GUARDIAN: Margaret Rogers
DATE: 1 Aug. 1836   AMOUNT OF BOND: $26,000
SECURITY: John Rogers   PAGE: 245
          James Hart

. . . .

ORPHAN: Alexander H., William A., Susan E., & Elizabeth A. Rogers
PARENT: Thornton Rogers   GUARDIAN: Margaret Rogers
DATE: 1 Aug. 1836   AMOUNT OF BOND: $26,000
SECURITY: John Rogers   PAGE: 247
          James Hart

[page 248 is blank]

II, pages 251 thru 259

ORPHAN: Caroline Nelson
PARENT: Hugh Nelson GUARDIAN: Thomas W. Meriwether
DATE: 3 Oct. 1836 AMOUNT OF BOND: $20,000
SECURITY: William D. Meriwether PAGE: 251

. . . .

ORPHAN: Keating S., & Robert W. Nelson
PARENT: Hugh Nelson GUARDIAN: Francis K. Nelson
DATE: 3 Oct. 1836 AMOUNT OF BOND: $20,000
SECURITY: William C. Rives PAGE: 253
James Lindsay

. . . .

ORPHAN: Calvin., Percilla., & Celestria Kinsolving
PARENT: Maddison B. Kinsolving GUARDIAN: John B. Watts
DATE: 3 Oct. 1836 AMOUNT OF BOND: $600
SECURITY: William Woods PAGE: 255

. . . .

ORPHAN: James Merritt
PARENT: Nicholas Merritt GUARDIAN: Caleb S. Abell
DATE: 8 Nov. 1836 AMOUNT OF BOND: $1,000
SECURITY: Markwood Merritt PAGE: 257

. . . .

ORPHAN: Thomas M. R. Bankhead
PARENT: Charles L. Bankhead GUARDIAN: Lewis Randolph
DATE: 8 Nov. 1836 AMOUNT OF BOND: $25,000
SECURITY: Thomas J. Randolph PAGE: 259

II, pages 261 thru 271

ORPHAN: John, Rebecca, Elizabeth, & Martha Gilmore
PARENT: William Gilmore   GUARDIAN: Peter Porter
DATE: 8 Nov. 1836   AMOUNT OF BOND: $8,000
SECURITY: George W. Kinsolving   PAGE: 261
          John Witt

. . . [PAGE 263 APPOINTS GUARDIAN FOR INCOMPETENT, Sarah Thomerson]

ORPHAN: Samuel, Thomas, Dolly, & Susan Ham
PARENT: Elijah Ham   GUARDIAN: Granville Ham
DATE: 5 Dec. 1836   AMOUNT OF BOND: $1,500
SECURITY: Edward Fearneyhough   PAGE: 265

. . . .

ORPHAN: James, & Joab Ham
PARENT: Elijah Ham   GUARDIAN: Granville A. Ham
DATE: 5 Dec. 1836   AMOUNT OF BOND: $1,500
SECURITY: Edward Fearneyhough   PAGE: 267

. . . .

ORPHAN: Samuel S. Johnson
PARENT: Stephen Johnson   GUARDIAN: Isaac Hicks
DATE: 5 Dec. 1836   AMOUNT OF BOND: $1,800
SECURITY: Willis Day   PAGE: 269

. . . .

ORPHAN: Elizabeth S., & Sally H. Davis
PARENT: Isaac Davis, Jr.   GUARDIAN: Garland Garth
DATE: 2 Jan. 1837   AMOUNT OF BOND: $24,000
SECURITY: Seth Burnley,   PAGE: 271
Richard Duke, Burwell G. Garth

ORPHAN: Cornelia D. Davis
PARENT: Isaac Davis, Jr.   GUARDIAN: Garland Garth
DATE: 2 Jan. 1837   AMOUNT OF BOND: $12,000
SECURITY: Richard Duke,   PAGE: 273
Seth Burnley, Burwell G. Garth

. . . .

ORPHAN: James, William, & Reuben Lindsay
PARENT: Reuben Lindsay   GUARDIAN: Mary M. Lindsay
DATE: 2 Jan. 1837   AMOUNT OF BOND: $10,000
SECURITY: Craven Peyton   PAGE: 275

. . . .

ORPHAN: Ann Lindsay [over 14 years of age]
PARENT: Reuben Lindsay   GUARDIAN: [mother] Mary M. Lindsay
DATE: 2 Jan. 1837   AMOUNT OF BOND: $5,000
SECURITY: Craven Peyton   PAGE: 277

. . . .

ORPHAN: Martha R. Duke
PARENT: John Duke   GUARDIAN: Charles W. Taylor
DATE: 6 Feb. 1837   AMOUNT OF BOND: $200
SECURITY: Alphonzo Garner   PAGE: 279
James Atkison

. . . .

ORPHAN: Richard Hall
PARENT: John Hall   GUARDIAN: Matthew W. Brown
DATE: 6 Feb. 1837   AMOUNT OF BOND: $4,000
SECURITY: Elisha Thurmond   PAGE: 281

II, pages 283 thru 291

ORPHAN: Tyre, John, Nicholas, Martha, Mary Ann, & Sally Dollins
PARENT: Jeremiah Dollins   GUARDIAN: [father] Jeremiah Dollins
DATE: 6 Feb. 1837   AMOUNT OF BOND: $1,000
SECURITY: John A. Foster   PAGE: 283

. . . .

ORPHAN: William D. Hall
PARENT: John Hall   GUARDIAN: Elisha Thurmond
DATE: 6 Feb. 1837   AMOUNT OF BOND: $4,000
SECURITY: Matthew Brown   PAGE: 285
          John Davis

. . . .

ORPHAN: Joshua W. Johnson
PARENT: William L. Johnson   GUARDIAN: Daniel Via
DATE: 6 Feb. 1837   AMOUNT OF BOND: $1,000
SECURITY: Gabriel Harper   PAGE: 287

. . . .

ORPHAN: William M. Morris
PARENT: William Morris   GUARDIAN: Marcus Durrett
DATE: 6 Feb. 1837   AMOUNT OF BOND: $20,000
SECURITY: Henry C. Moore,   PAGE: 289
George M. Woods, George W. Harris,
Larkin Hudson

. . . .

ORPHAN: William G. W. Cheatham
PARENT: William Cheatham   GUARDIAN: Sarah Cheatham
DATE: 9 March 1837   AMOUNT OF BOND: $2,000
SECURITY: Ezriah M. Wolfe   PAGE: 291

II, pages 293 thru 301

ORPHAN:	Mary P., & Mildred P. Moon		
PARENT:	Littleberry Moon	GUARDIAN:	Samuel O. Moon
DATE:	3 April 1837	AMOUNT OF BOND:	$10,000
SECURITY:	Edward H. Moon Thomas Jackson	PAGE:	293

. . . .

ORPHAN:	Marshall Piper		
PARENT:	William Piper	GUARDIAN:	Willis W. Piper
DATE:	3 April 1837	AMOUNT OF BOND:	$4,000
SECURITY:	Jeremiah White Richard M. Durrett	PAGE:	295

. . . .

ORPHAN:	Sarah Ann Sims		
PARENT:	Isaac Sims	GUARDIAN:	Bluford Sims
DATE:	3 July 1837	AMOUNT OF BOND:	$2,000
SECURITY:	Richard D. Sims Michael Catterton, Sr.	PAGE:	297

. . . .

ORPHAN:	Sarah, & Ellen Newcomb		
PARENT:	John Newcomb	GUARDIAN:	Nathan C. Goodman
DATE:	10 Aug. 1837	AMOUNT OF BOND:	$600
SECURITY:	Joseph Dettor	PAGE:	299

. . . .

ORPHAN:	Elizabeth Caroline Bishop		
PARENT:	William Bishop	GUARDIAN:	Joseph Essex
DATE:	4 Sept. 1837	AMOUNT OF BOND:	$300
SECURITY:	John Dettor	PAGE:	301

II, pages 303 thru 309

ORPHAN: John N. C., & Catharine M. Stockton
PARENT: John N. C. Stockton   GUARDIAN: William T. Stockton
DATE: 4 Sept. 1837   AMOUNT OF BOND: $40,000
SECURITY: Richard C. Stockton   PAGE: 303

. . . .

ORPHAN: Gay Ferguson Carr
PARENT: John A. Carr   GUARDIAN: Samuel Carr
DATE: 2 Oct. 1837   AMOUNT OF BOND: $4,000
SECURITY: John A. G. Davis   PAGE: 304

. . . .

[copy of a bond of Hardin County, Kentucky]
ORPHAN: Waller, John, George W., Ira T., & Charles F. Bailey
PARENT: John H. Bailey   GUARDIAN: [father] John H. Bailey
DATE: 12 Oct. 1839 [copy]   AMOUNT OF BOND: $1,600
SECURITY: William Smith   PAGE: 305
          Albert Bailey

These children are by John H. Bailey's wife Polly Bailey late Polly Goodin, & are legatees of grandfather William Goodin, late of Virgin:

ORPHAN: Catharine Virginia, & Maria Louisa Brand
PARENT: Chiles M. Brand   GUARDIAN: Nimrod Bramham
DATE: 2 Oct. 1837   AMOUNT OF BOND: $700
SECURITY: Chapman W. Maupin   PAGE: 307

. . . .

[counter security ordered given in this case]
ORPHAN: William M. Morris
PARENT: William Morris   GUARDIAN: Ann D. Rodes, formerly
                                             Ann D. Morris
DATE: 2 Oct. 1837   AMOUNT OF BOND: $20,000
SECURITY: John D. Rodes,   PAGE: 309
John Rodes, George W. Kinsolving, Chapman W. Maupin, William Rodes,
Edmund J. Thompson, Nathan C. Goodman, Charles Brown, Bezaleel Brown,
Boswell P. Yates

II, pages 311 thru 319

ORPHAN: George M., Jackson M., & David Terrell
PARENT: Reuben Terrell   GUARDIAN: Susan Terrell
DATE: 3 Sept. 1838   AMOUNT OF BOND: $2,000
SECURITY: James W. Poindexter PAGE: 311

. . . .

ORPHAN: Elizabeth, Ann, Reuben, Mildred, Rebecca, & William Thomas
PARENT: Reuben Thomas   GUARDIAN: Mary Thomas
DATE: 2 Oct. 1837   AMOUNT OF BOND: $2,500
SECURITY: John Eubank   PAGE: 313

. . . .

ORPHAN: John, William, Henry, & Mary Wren
PARENT: William Wren   GUARDIAN: Stapleton C. Sneed
DATE: 2 Oct. 1837   AMOUNT OF BOND: $1,000
SECURITY: Frederick Gillum   PAGE: 315

. . . .

ORPHAN: Francis L., Elizabeth, & Julia Thacker
PARENT: Wilson Thacker   GUARDIAN: Mary B. Thacker
DATE: 5 Nov. 1838   AMOUNT OF BOND: $2,000
SECURITY: Matthew Wingfield   PAGE: 317

. . . .

ORPHAN: Ann J., John W., & Richart T. McLeod
PARENT: William McLeod   GUARDIAN: Belinda McLeod
DATE: 7 Nov. 1837   AMOUNT OF BOND: $20,000
SECURITY: John Jeffries   PAGE: 319

II, pages 321 thru 329

ORPHAN: Elizabeth L. Ames
PARENT: Samuel B. Ames   **GUARDIAN:** Eli Ames
DATE: 4 Dec. 1837   **AMOUNT OF BOND:** $50
SECURITY: Nathan J. Barnett   **PAGE:** 321

. . . .

ORPHAN: John A. Carr
PARENT: John A. Carr   **GUARDIAN:** Ellen M. Carr
DATE: 4 Dec. 1837   **AMOUNT OF BOND:** $4,000
SECURITY: Samuel Carr   **PAGE:** 323
Joseph W. Morris

. . . .

ORPHAN: Amanda M. Herndon
PARENT: Reuben Herndon   **GUARDIAN:** John M. Herndon
DATE: 5 Dec. 1837   **AMOUNT OF BOND:** $2,000
SECURITY: Jesse B. Hamner   **PAGE:** 325
Nelson W. Elsom

. . . .

ORPHAN: Mary Ann, & Eliza Wheeler
PARENT: Joshua Wheeler   **GUARDIAN:** Joshua N. Wheeler
DATE: 4 Feb. 1839   **AMOUNT OF BOND:** $4,000
SECURITY: Micajah Wheeler   **PAGE:** 327
John Wheeler

. . . .

ORPHAN: Mildred L., & Mary Ann J. Wood
PARENT: Thomas Wood   **GUARDIAN:** John Fray
DATE: 1 Jan. 1838   **AMOUNT OF BOND:** $14,000
SECURITY: Nelson Barksdale   **PAGE:** 329

II, pages 331 thru 339

ORPHAN: Alfred C. Wood

PARENT: Thomas Wood GUARDIAN: John Fray

DATE: 1 Jan. 1838 AMOUNT OF BOND: $7,000

SECURITY: Nelson Barksdale PAGE: 331

. . . .

ORPHAN: John P., Thomas W., Chapman J., Mary J. M., Francis D., & Franklin J. Michie

PARENT: Jonathan Michie GUARDIAN: William Michie

DATE: 6 March 1838 AMOUNT OF BOND: $15,000

SECURITY: James Michie PAGE: 333
John E. Michie

. . . .

ORPHAN: Eugene Davis

PARENT: John A. G. Davis GUARDIAN: [father] John A. G. Davis

DATE: 2 April 1838 AMOUNT OF BOND: $600

SECURITY: Frank Carr PAGE: 335

. . . .

[EXECUTOR'S BOND]

DECEASED: Samuel Cobbs

EXECUTOR: James R. Watson

DATE: 5 June 1838 AMOUNT OF BOND: $8,000

SECURITY: John Watson PAGE: 337
Frank Carr

. . . .

ORPHAN: Warwick W. Hamner and John Moore

PARENT: [none given] GUARDIAN: William Donaho

DATE: 4 June 1838 AMOUNT OF BOND: $5,000

SECURITY: Thomas Burton PAGE: 339

II, pages 341 thru 349

ORPHAN: Ebenezer Goss

PARENT: John Goss GUARDIAN: John W. Goss

DATE: 6 Aug. 1838 AMOUNT OF BOND: $20,000

SECURITY: James W. Goss PAGE: 341
William W. Goss

. . . .

ORPHAN: Elizabeth Spencer

PARENT: William Spencer GUARDIAN: Michael Powell

DATE: 6 Aug. 1838 AMOUNT OF BOND: $50

SECURITY: David Hicks PAGE: 343

. . . .

ORPHAN: Elizabeth M., Mary M., Charlotte D., Anne M. W., & Martha L. Moon

PARENT: Jacob Moon GUARDIAN: Isaac D. Moon

DATE: 3 Sept. 1838 AMOUNT OF BOND: $10,000

SECURITY: John D. Moon, PAGE: 345
William H. Johnston, John H. Coleman

. . . .

ORPHAN: Lindsay Woodson

PARENT: Augustine Woodson GUARDIAN: Caleb S. Abell

DATE: 1 Oct. 1838 AMOUNT OF BOND: $100

SECURITY: Tucker Woodson PAGE: 347

. . . .

ORPHAN: Matilda, Lucy, Henry, & Albert Quarles

PARENT: Albert Quarles GUARDIAN: William W. Minor

DATE: 3 Dec. 1838 AMOUNT OF BOND: $28,000

SECURITY: John Minor PAGE: 349
Alexander Garrett

II, pages 351 thru 359

ORPHAN: Samuel, & William Thacker

PARENT: Martin[?] Thacker GUARDIAN: Mildred Thacker

DATE: 3 Dec. 1838 AMOUNT OF BOND: $2,000

SECURITY: Benjamin Pace PAGE: 351
James King, John M. Wingfield

. . . .

ORPHAN: Margaret N. Gibbons [over 14 years of age]

PARENT: John M. Gibbons GUARDIAN: Lucy Brockenbrough
[late of Richmond]
DATE: 7 Jan. 1839 AMOUNT OF BOND: $100

SECURITY: James W. Saunders PAGE: 353

. . . .

ORPHAN: Meredith, Delitha, & Henry Mundy

PARENT: Archibald Mundy GUARDIAN: Madison Dowell

DATE: 7 Jan. 1839 AMOUNT OF BOND: $500

SECURITY: John J. Bowcock PAGE: 355

. . . .

ORPHAN: Horace, Elizabeth, Lilbourn, Frances, Harriot, & Thomas Shifl

PARENT: Anderson R. Shiflett GUARDIAN: Catharine M. Shiflett

DATE: 4 Feb. 1839 AMOUNT OF BOND: $60,000

SECURITY: Benjamin Sneed PAGE: 357
Stapleton C. Sneed

. . . .

ORPHAN: Joseph, & Henrietta Shiflett

PARENT: Anderson R. Shiflett GUARDIAN: Benjamin Sneed

DATE: 4 Feb. 1839 AMOUNT OF BOND: $20,000

SECURITY: Stapleton C. Sneed PAGE: 359
Collin Johnson

II, pages 361 thru 369

ORPHAN: William N. Ragland
PARENT: John C. Ragland GUARDIAN: John K. Regland
DATE: 1 April 1839 AMOUNT OF BOND: $15,000
SECURITY: John R. Ragland PAGE: 361

. . . .

ORPHAN: Frances Ann Cobbs
PARENT: Samuel Cobbs GUARDIAN: Daniel L. Maupin
DATE: 6 May 1839 AMOUNT OF BOND: $800
SECURITY: David Maupin PAGE: 363

. . . .

ORPHAN: Samuel, Thomas, Doratha, & Susan Ham
PARENT: Elijah Ham GUARDIAN: Edward Ham
DATE: 3 June 1839 AMOUNT OF BOND: $4,000
SECURITY: Edward Fearneyhough PAGE: 365
Thomas Gilbert

. . . .

ORPHAN: John A. Carr
PARENT: John A. Carr GUARDIAN: James L. Carr
DATE: 1 July 1839 AMOUNT OF BOND: $5,000
SECURITY: Samuel Carr PAGE: 367

. . . .

ORPHAN: Sarah Elizabeth McCord
PARENT: Alexander McCord GUARDIAN: Elizabeth J. McCord
DATE: 1 July 1839 AMOUNT OF BOND: $500
SECURITY: Ambrose Maupin PAGE: 369

II, pages 371 thru 379

ORPHAN:	Ann Eliza, Frances J., Schuyler A., Mary S., & Samuel J. Hart		
PARENT:	Sophia Hart	GUARDIAN:	James Hart
DATE:	5 Aug. 1839	AMOUNT OF BOND:	$2,000
SECURITY:	William D. Hart	PAGE:	371

. . . .

ORPHAN:	Sarah Ann Wilhoit		
PARENT:	Ezekiel Wilhoit	GUARDIAN:	Ezekiel Wilhoit
DATE:	5 Aug. 1839	AMOUNT OF BOND:	$6,000
SECURITY:	Robert U. Brooking John Fray	PAGE:	373

. . . .

ORPHAN:	Martha Jane Wilhoit		
PARENT:	Ezekiel Wilhoit	GUARDIAN:	Ezekiel Wilhoit
DATE:	5 Aug. 1839	AMOUNT OF BOND:	$6,000
SECURITY:	Robert U. Brooking John Fray	PAGE:	375

. . . .

ORPHAN:	Frances, & Fleming Moon		
PARENT:	Jacob Moon	GUARDIAN:	Nathaniel Moon
DATE:	2 Sept. 1839	AMOUNT OF BOND:	$1,500
SECURITY:	John H. Coleman	PAGE:	377

. . . .

ORPHAN:	Caroline M. Salmon		
PARENT:	Thomas Salmon	GUARDIAN:	Thomas R. Dunn
DATE:	2 Sept. 1839	AMOUNT OF BOND:	$8,000
SECURITY:	Ira B. Brown James Early	PAGE:	379

ORPHAN: Mary E. Warwick
PARENT: Andrew S. Warwick GUARDIAN: William Woods
DATE: 2 Sept. 1839 AMOUNT OF BOND: $12,000
SECURITY: George M. Woods PAGE: 381

. . . .

ORPHAN: Catharine A. Clarke
PARENT: Thomas N. Clarke GUARDIAN: Willis D. Garth
DATE: 7 Oct. 1839 AMOUNT OF BOND: $1,000
SECURITY: Henry C. Moore PAGE: 383

. . . .

ORPHAN: Thomas Jones
PARENT: James Jones GUARDIAN: Mary Jones
DATE: 7 Oct. 1839 AMOUNT OF BOND: $1,200
SECURITY: Lewis Bailey, PAGE: 385
Charles M. Bailey, John Martin

. . . .

ORPHAN: Sarah Shiflett
PARENT: Anderson R. Shiflett GUARDIAN: Benjamin Sneed
DATE: 7 Oct. 1839 AMOUNT OF BOND: $5,000
SECURITY: Stapleton C. Sneed PAGE: 387

. . . .

ORPHAN: Martha Walker
PARENT: Laurence[?] Walker GUARDIAN: Thompson Herndon
DATE: 7 Oct. 1839 AMOUNT OF BOND: $100
SECURITY: Thomas Burton PAGE: 389

II, pages 391 thru 399

ORPHAN: Waller, John, George W., Ira T., & Charles C. Bailey
PARENT: John H. Bailey **GUARDIAN:** [father] John H. Bailey
DATE: 4 Nov. 1839 **AMOUNT OF BOND:** $2,000
SECURITY: Albert Bailey **PAGE:** 391
Lewis Teel, William Woods

. . . .

ORPHAN: Elizabeth Lane
PARENT: William Lane **GUARDIAN:** Tarlton Via
DATE: 2 Dec. 1839 **AMOUNT OF BOND:** $200
SECURITY: Reuben Via **PAGE:** 393

. . . .

ORPHAN: Christopher T. Smith
PARENT: Jacob Smith **GUARDIAN:** Thomas Burton
DATE: 2 Dec. 1839 **AMOUNT OF BOND:** $100
SECURITY: Benjamin M. Perkins **PAGE:** 395

. . . .

ORPHAN: Thomas, James, & Robert Baber
PARENT: James Baber **GUARDIAN:** William Powell
DATE: 6 Jan. 1840 **AMOUNT OF BOND:** $1,000
SECURITY: Benjamin Thurmond, **PAGE:** 397
Turner Thurmond, John Bowman

. . . .

ORPHAN: Mary C. Wingfield
PARENT: John B. Wingfield **GUARDIAN:** Richard Wingfield
DATE: 6 Jan. 1840 **AMOUNT OF BOND:** $2,000
SECURITY: James T. Early **PAGE:** 399

II, pages 401 thru 409

ORPHAN:	Louisa, & Virginia Cobbs		
PARENT:	Samuel Cobbs	GUARDIAN:	James R. Watson
DATE:	2 March 1840	AMOUNT OF BOND:	$2,400
SECURITY:	John Watson	PAGE:	401

. . . .

ORPHAN:	Elijah, Elizabeth, Lilbourn, Merial[?], & William L. Hughes		
PARENT:	William Hughes [not deceased]	GUARDIAN:	Frances E. Hughes
DATE:	2 March 1840	AMOUNT OF BOND:	$200
SECURITY:	Lewis Teel	PAGE:	403

. . . .

ORPHAN:	John William Haws		
PARENT:	Daniel Haws	GUARDIAN:	William P. Farish
DATE:	3 March 1840	AMOUNT OF BOND:	$100
SECURITY:	Benjamin Ficklin	PAGE:	405

. . . .

ORPHAN:	Telitha Ann, & Meredith Mundy		
PARENT:	Archy Mundy	GUARDIAN:	Mary Mundy
DATE:	2 March 1840	AMOUNT OF BOND:	$4,000
SECURITY:	John Wilkerson	PAGE:	407

. . . .

ORPHAN:	Malinda F. Spencer an illegitimate child		
PARENT:		GUARDIAN:	Claiborne Rice
DATE:	2 March 1840	AMOUNT OF BOND:	$100
SECURITY:	Thomas Angel	PAGE:	409

II, pages 411 thru 419

ORPHAN:	William H., Francis, & Sarah Ann Elizabeth Wood		
PARENT:	James Wood	GUARDIAN:	Rebecca Wood
DATE:	2 March 1840	AMOUNT OF BOND:	$1,550
SECURITY:	Henry Marshall Jacob C. Lupton	PAGE:	411

. . . .

ORPHAN:	Lucinda, & Henry Wood		
PARENT:	James Wood	GUARDIAN:	Rebecca Wood
DATE:	2 March 1840	AMOUNT OF BOND:	$625
SECURITY:	Henry Marshall Jacob C. Lupton	PAGE:	413

. . . .

ORPHAN:	Mary M., & Virginia L., [over 14 years of age], Lucy Ellen, & Maria Minor		
PARENT:	Warner W. Minor	GUARDIAN:	Lucian Minor
DATE:	6 April 1840	AMOUNT OF BOND:	$10,000
SECURITY:	John Timberlake William Wertenbaker	PAGE:	415

. . . .

ORPHAN:	Willey[?] Jane Woodson		
PARENT:	William D. Woodson	GUARDIAN:	Lucy T. Woodson
DATE:	6 April 1840	AMOUNT OF BOND:	$1,000
SECURITY:	Thomas Ammonett	PAGE:	417

. . . .

ORPHAN:	Clement R., Martha, Andrew J., & Ann Maria Seay		
PARENT:	Peter H. Seay	GUARDIAN:	George L. Seay
DATE:	2 June 1840	AMOUNT OF BOND:	$5,000
SECURITY:	Martin Tutwiler	PAGE:	419

II, pages 421 thru 429

ORPHAN: Jane, Adeline, Frances, William H., & Columbia Durrett
PARENT: Thomas Durrett   GUARDIAN: William Catterton, Jr.
DATE: 6 July 1840   AMOUNT OF BOND: [left blank]
SECURITY: Marcus Durrett   PAGE: 421

. . . .

ORPHAN: Robert C., George C., & James Henry Rives
PARENT: George Rives   GUARDIAN: [father] George Rives
DATE: 6 July 1840   AMOUNT OF BOND: $300
SECURITY: Alexander Rives   PAGE: 423

. . . .

ORPHAN: Ann Lyon [over 14 years of age]
PARENT: Samuel Lyon   GUARDIAN: William D. Fitch
DATE: 3 Aug. 1840   AMOUNT OF BOND: $100
SECURITY: Lewis Sowell   PAGE: 425

. . . .

ORPHAN: Joseph A., James H., Mary Jane, & Richard J. Grinstead
PARENT: James H. Grinstead   GUARDIAN: Sarah Grinstead
DATE: 5 Oct. 1840   AMOUNT OF BOND: $10,000
SECURITY: John Eagan,   PAGE: 427
Bailey Shumate, Joseph Dettor,
William G. Barksdale

. . . .

ORPHAN: John D., Nicholas D., Louisa Jane,
           Sarah Ann, & James J. Hays
PARENT: William Hays   GUARDIAN: William Hays
DATE: 1 March 1841   AMOUNT OF BOND: $250
SECURITY: Benjamin Wheeler   PAGE: 429

ORPHAN: Elizabeth, Franklin, Letty Ann, & Arthur E. Wheat

PARENT: Elijah T. Wheat   GUARDIAN: Rezen[?] Wheat

DATE: 1 March 1841   AMOUNT OF BOND: $1,500

SECURITY: Thomas J. Randolph   PAGE: 431

. . . .

ORPHAN: Jesse T. Garth

PARENT: Jesse Garth   GUARDIAN: Jesse Garth

DATE: 5 April 1841   AMOUNT OF BOND: $1,600

SECURITY: Bezaleel Brown   PAGE: 433

. . . .

ORPHAN: Thomas H. Gay

PARENT: Thomas Gay [not deceased]   GUARDIAN: Samuel S. Gay

DATE: 5 April 1841   AMOUNT OF BOND: $350

SECURITY: Jesse Lobban
John Eubank   PAGE: 435

. . . .

ORPHAN: Nicholas, Catharine, William, Euster[?], John, Martha, & Elizabeth Shultz

PARENT: John Shultz, Sr.   GUARDIAN: [father] John Shultz,

DATE: 5 April 1841   AMOUNT OF BOND: $700

SECURITY: Joseph Dettor   PAGE: 437

. . . .

ORPHAN: Mary[?] Ann Thurmond

PARENT: John Thurmond   GUARDIAN: James Rittenhouse

DATE: 5 April 1841   AMOUNT OF BOND: $5,000

SECURITY: Henry Rittenhouse   PAGE: 439

II, pages 441 thru 449

ORPHAN: Joseph, James, Richard, & Jane Grinstead

PARENT: James H. Grinstead GUARDIAN: John Eagan

DATE: 3 May 1841 AMOUNT OF BOND: $10,000

SECURITY: Sampson Eagan, PAGE: 441
Bailey Shumate, Jechonias Yancey

. . . .

ORPHAN: Beatriss Pence

PARENT: Alexander Pence GUARDIAN: William D. Fitch

DATE: 3 May 1841 AMOUNT OF BOND: $100

SECURITY: John Cochran PAGE: 443

. . . .

ORPHAN: John Gay Carr

PARENT: Lieut. John A. Carr GUARDIAN: James L. Carr

DATE: 5 July 1841 AMOUNT OF BOND: $5,000

SECURITY: Samuel Carr PAGE: 445

. . . .

ORPHAN: Nancy T. Moore
an illegitimate child
PARENT: of Patsy Thacker GUARDIAN: Benjamin Moore

DATE: 7 June 1841 AMOUNT OF BOND: $100

SECURITY: William L. Wash PAGE: 447

. . . .

ORPHAN: Robert Sneed

PARENT: Nicholas Sneed GUARDIAN: Benjamin Moore

DATE: 9 June 1841 AMOUNT OF BOND: $100

SECURITY: William L. Wash PAGE: 449

II, pages 451 thru 459

ORPHAN: Thursday Jenetta Hilton

PARENT: William Hilton   **GUARDIAN:** Joel W. Brown

DATE: 3 Aug. 1841   **AMOUNT OF BOND:** $200

SECURITY: William W. Dawson   **PAGE:** 451

. . . .

ORPHAN: Martha Hay Leitch

PARENT: Samuel Leitch   **GUARDIAN:** James A. Leitch

DATE: 3 Aug. 1841   **AMOUNT OF BOND:** $6,000

SECURITY: William W. Dawson   **PAGE:** 453
Andrew Sample

. . . .

ORPHAN: Benjamin J. [10 years old], & Mary E. [7 years old] Wheeler

PARENT: Micajah W. Wheeler   **GUARDIAN:** Joshua W. Abell

DATE: 2 Aug. 1841   **AMOUNT OF BOND:** $4,000

SECURITY: John Woodson   **PAGE:** 455
John T. Wood

The mother of these two orphans was Julia[?] Ann Wheeler

. . . .

ORPHAN: Ann Lindsay

PARENT: Reuben Lindsay   **GUARDIAN:** Stephen F. Sampson

DATE: 6 Sept. 1841   **AMOUNT OF BOND:** $5,000

SECURITY: William W. Dawson   **PAGE:** 457

. . . .

ORPHAN: James, William, & Reuben Lindsay

PARENT: Reuben Lindsay   **GUARDIAN:** Nathan C. Goodman

DATE: 4 Oct. 1841   **AMOUNT OF BOND:** $18,000

SECURITY: William Goodman   **PAGE:** 459

II, pages 461 thru 469

ORPHAN: Thomas J. Wertenbaker
PARENT: William Wertenbaker   GUARDIAN: [father] William Wertenbaker
DATE: 5 Oct. 1841   AMOUNT OF BOND: $1,000
SECURITY: Michael Johnson   PAGE: 461

. . . .

ORPHAN: Samuel G. White
PARENT: Henry White   GUARDIAN: [father] Henry White
DATE: 5 Oct. 1841   AMOUNT OF BOND: $1,200
SECURITY: Francis McGehee   PAGE: 463

. . . .

ORPHAN: Martha Ann, John W., James W., Nicholas M., Sarah C., & Henry K. Dettor
PARENT: Matthias[?] Dettor   GUARDIAN: James W. Suddarth
DATE: 2 Nov. 1841   AMOUNT OF BOND: $8,000
SECURITY: William H. Suddarth   PAGE: 465

. . . .

ORPHAN: Sarah Mildred, & Thomas Rothwell
PARENT: Anderson Rothwell   GUARDIAN: Thomas Foster
DATE: 1 Nov. 1841   AMOUNT OF BOND: $500
SECURITY: William H. Brown   PAGE: 467

. . . .

ORPHAN: James A., & Catharine A. Trice [over 14 years of age]
PARENT: Jefferson E. Trice   GUARDIAN: [uncle] Merewether L. Anderson
DATE: 1 Nov. 1841   AMOUNT OF BOND: $8,000
SECURITY: Thomas Macon   PAGE: 469

The fact that Merewether L. Anderson is the uncle of these orphans, and that they are over 14, is found on page 398 of this volume.

ORPHAN: Mary M., Charlotte D., Anna Maria, J. W., & Martha L. Moon
PARENT: Jacob Moon   GUARDIAN: John D. Moon, Jr.
DATE: 6 Dec. 1841   AMOUNT OF BOND: $12,00
SECURITY: John H. Coleman   PAGE: 471
          Edward H. Moon

. . . .

ORPHAN: Jonathan B., Benjamin F., & Keziah S. Rogers
PARENT: Thompson Rogers   GUARDIAN: [father] Thompson Rogers
DATE: 6 Dec. 1841   AMOUNT OF BOND: $600
SECURITY: Cosby M. Robertson PAGE: 473

. . . .

ORPHAN: Lindsay Thacker
PARENT: Celia Thacker   GUARDIAN: Benjamin Moore
DATE: 6 Dec. 1841   AMOUNT OF BOND: $100
SECURITY: James W. Wedderfield PAGE: 475

. . . .

ORPHAN: Josias Ricks
PARENT: Gilbert Ricks   GUARDIAN: George C. Gilmer
DATE: 3 Jan. 1842   AMOUNT OF BOND: $100
SECURITY: John H. Gilmer   PAGE: 477

. . . .

ORPHAN: James Carver
PARENT: Reuben Carver   GUARDIAN: William D. Hart
DATE: 7 Feb. 1842   AMOUNT OF BOND: $2,000
SECURITY: John Eubank, Sr.   PAGE: 479

II, pages 481 thru 489

ORPHAN:	Elizabeth E. Gilmore		
PARENT:	William Gilmore	**GUARDIAN:**	Boswell P. Yates
DATE:	7 Feb. 1842	**AMOUNT OF BOND:**	$1,200
SECURITY:	Thomas C. Yates Edward Wingfield	**PAGE:**	481

. . . .

ORPHAN:	Casper Powell		
PARENT:	Samuel Powell	**GUARDIAN:**	Samuel M. Powell
DATE:	7 Feb. 1842	**AMOUNT OF BOND:**	$1,200
SECURITY:	Richard S. Abell	**PAGE:**	483

. . . .

ORPHAN:	Martha Gilmore		
PARENT:	William Gilmore	**GUARDIAN:**	Thomas C. Yates
DATE:	7 March 1842	**AMOUNT OF BOND:**	$800
SECURITY:	John E. Gilmore John W. Fenwick	**PAGE:**	485

. . . .

ORPHAN:	Louisa Jane, & Evaline Bolling, [over 14 years of age], Elizabeth F., & Lucy T. Pace		
PARENT:	Henry T. Pace	**GUARDIAN:**	John Mosby
DATE:	7 March 1842	**AMOUNT OF BOND:**	$6,000
SECURITY:	Benjamin Mosby Joseph Pace	**PAGE:**	487

. . . .

ORPHAN:	Eliza R. Norris		
PARENT:	Opie Norris	**GUARDIAN:**	Egbert R. Watson
DATE:	2 May 1842	**AMOUNT OF BOND:**	$5,000
SECURITY:	James Norris	**PAGE:**	489

ORPHAN: George G. Spiller
PARENT: Colin C. Spiller   GUARDIAN: George C. Gilmer
DATE: 6 June 1842   AMOUNT OF BOND: $1,000
SECURITY: Zachariah R. Lewis   PAGE: 491

. . . .

ORPHAN: Mary W. Digges
PARENT: George P. Digges   GUARDIAN: Malinda Digges
DATE: 4 July 1842   AMOUNT OF BOND: $400
SECURITY: David Michie   PAGE: 493
          Michael Catterton

. . . .

ORPHAN: Martha Woodson,
          an illegitimate child
PARENT: GUARDIAN: West[?] Langford
DATE: 4 July 1842   AMOUNT OF BOND: $100
SECURITY: Anderson Langford   PAGE: 495

. . . .

ORPHAN: Theodore, Henry, & Martha Rothwell
PARENT: Harriet C. Jeffries,   GUARDIAN: William Jeffries
     late Harriet C. Rothwell
DATE: 5 Sept. 1842   AMOUNT OF BOND: $2,000
SECURITY: James Jeffries   PAGE: 497

. . . .

ORPHAN: John Minor, Jr.
PARENT: James Minor   GUARDIAN: Lucy C. Terrell
DATE: 8 Nov. 1842   AMOUNT OF BOND: $3,000
SECURITY: Dabney Minor   PAGE: 499

II, pages 500 thru 507

ORPHAN: Virginia F., Sarah A., & Samantha S. Brown, [over 14]; [in pencil: James L., Jacintha C., & Angeline M. Brown]

PARENT: Ira B. Brown GUARDIAN: [brother] Burlington B. Brown

DATE: 29 Sept. 1842 AMOUNT OF BOND: [none given]

SECURITY: [none given] PAGE: 500

This material appeared in a handwritten choice of guardian request, rather than in a regular bond. See also page 537.
. . . .

ORPHAN: Elizabeth E., & Henry O. Austin [over 14 years of age]

PARENT: Obediah Austin GUARDIAN: [uncle] John H. Barksdale

DATE: 5 Dec. 1842 AMOUNT OF BOND: $6,000

SECURITY: Francis L. Austin PAGE: 501
John T. Austin

Francis Birckhead, who was appointed their guardian in 1835, surrenders guardianship.
. . . .

ORPHAN: Mary Elizabeth, Horace Buckner, & Martha George Johnston

PARENT: Richard H. Johnston GUARDIAN: Joseph W. Twyman

DATE: 2 Jan. 1843 AMOUNT OF BOND: $5,000

SECURITY: Nathaniel Burnley, PAGE: 503
James F. Burnley, William Goodman

. . . .

ORPHAN: Robert N. Payne

PARENT: Nathaniel W. Payne GUARDIAN: [father] Nathaniel W. Payne

DATE: 2 Jan. 1843 AMOUNT OF BOND: $2,500

SECURITY: William. T. Higgen- PAGE: 505
botham

. . . .

ORPHAN: William C. Burton

PARENT: William C. Burton GUARDIAN: James A. Watson

DATE: 6 Feb. 1843 AMOUNT OF BOND: $2,500

SECURITY: Thomas R. Bailey PAGE: 507

ORPHAN: Joseph T. Johnston
PARENT: Richard H. Johnston   **GUARDIAN:** Joseph W. Twyman
DATE: 6 Feb. 1843   **AMOUNT OF BOND:** $1,500
SECURITY: Thomas Ballard   **PAGE:** 509

. . . .

ORPHAN: William H. Rice
PARENT: Holeman Rice   **GUARDIAN:** Samuel A. Leake
DATE: 6 March 1843   **AMOUNT OF BOND:** $100
SECURITY: Edward Wertenbaker   **PAGE:** 511

. . . .

ORPHAN: Samuel, Edward, Eliza, & Susan Dyer
PARENT: Samuel Dyer, Jr.   **GUARDIAN:** Thomas B. Dyer
DATE: 3 April 1843   **AMOUNT OF BOND:** $1,200
SECURITY: George B. Payne   **PAGE:** 513
Robert Dyer

. . . .

ORPHAN: Sarah Laughlin
PARENT: Thomas C. Laughlin   **GUARDIAN:** William P. Farish
DATE: 3 April 1843   **AMOUNT OF BOND:** $500
SECURITY: Lewis Sowell   **PAGE:** 519

. . . .

ORPHAN: Frances Ann Smith
PARENT: Jacob Smith   **GUARDIAN:** William T. Davis
DATE: 3 April 1843   **AMOUNT OF BOND:** $50
SECURITY: Hugh Davis   **PAGE:** 521

II, pages 523 thru 531

ORPHAN: Mary E. Woodson
PARENT: Stephen Woodson   **GUARDIAN:** Peter White
DATE: 3 April 1843   AMOUNT OF BOND: $3,000
SECURITY: Benjamin H. Magruder   PAGE: 523

. . . .

ORPHAN: Alonzo, Marcellus J., Chasteau, & Henrietta A. Wingfield
PARENT: John J. Wingfield   GUARDIAN: [father] John J. Wingfield
DATE: 5 June 1843   AMOUNT OF BOND: $2,500
SECURITY: Francis Wingfield   PAGE: 525

. . . .

ORPHAN: Betty [Elizabeth] Lewis Minor
PARENT: Samuel O. Minor   GUARDIAN: James H. Terrell
DATE: 3 July 1843   AMOUNT OF BOND: $100
SECURITY: E. R. Watson   PAGE: 527

. . . .

ORPHAN: Frances, Virginia Ann, John James, Ludamon, Selina, & Rush Appleberry
PARENT: William S. Appleberry [not deceased]   GUARDIAN: Dabney Carr
DATE: 8 Aug. 1843   AMOUNT OF BOND: $2,000
SECURITY: William S. Appleberry   PAGE: 529
          Jordan Thurmond

. . . .

ORPHAN: Enock, & Amanda Gentry
PARENT: Amanda Gentry   GUARDIAN: Elisha C. Browning
DATE: 7 Aug. 1843   AMOUNT OF BOND: $700
SECURITY: John A. Foster   PAGE: 531

II, pages 533 thru 541

ORPHAN:	Sarah A., & Isaetta L. Hudson		
PARENT:	Charles Hudson	GUARDIAN:	Agness E. Hudson
DATE:	7 Aug. 1843	AMOUNT OF BOND:	$40,000
SECURITY:	Daniel Lewis Zac Lewis, Sr.	PAGE:	533

. . . .

ORPHAN:	Thomas Jones		
PARENT:	James W. Jones	GUARDIAN:	James O. Hawley
DATE:	7 Aug. 1843	AMOUNT OF BOND:	$1,200
SECURITY:	Lewis B. Bailey	PAGE:	535

. . . .

ORPHAN:	Virginia F., & Sarah A. Brown		
PARENT:	Ira B. Brown	GUARDIAN:	Benjamin T. Brown
DATE:	4 Sept. 1843	AMOUNT OF BOND:	$4,000
SECURITY:	Edmund Davis	PAGE:	537

. . . .

ORPHAN:	Samantha S. Brown		
PARENT:	Ira B. Brown	GUARDIAN:	William R. Roberts
DATE:	4 Sept. 1843	AMOUNT OF BOND:	$2,000
SECURITY:	Benjamin T. Brown, David Mills, M. R. Maupin	PAGE:	539

. . . .

ORPHAN:	Jacintha C., & Angelina M. Brown		
PARENT:	Ira B. Brown	GUARDIAN:	Bernard B. Thompson
DATE:	4 Sept. 1843	AMOUNT OF BOND:	$4,000
SECURITY:	Edmund J. Thompson	PAGE:	541

II, pages 543 thru 551

ORPHAN:	James L. Brown		
PARENT:	Ira B. Brown	GUARDIAN:	Thomas H. Brown
DATE:	4 Sept. 1843	AMOUNT OF BOND:	$2,000
SECURITY:	John J. Bowcock	PAGE:	543

. . . .

ORPHAN:	John W. Haws		
PARENT:	Daniel M. Haws	GUARDIAN:	John W. Chewning
DATE:	4 Sept. 1843	AMOUNT OF BOND:	$100
SECURITY:	William P. Farish	PAGE:	545

. . . .

ORPHAN:	Jane A. Smith		
PARENT:	Charles Smith	GUARDIAN:	Robert P. Smith
DATE:	2 Oct. 1843	AMOUNT OF BOND:	$5,000
SECURITY:	William Woods	PAGE:	547

. . . .

ORPHAN:	Sarah Mason		
PARENT:	Valentine M. Mason	GUARDIAN:	John H. Nicholas
DATE:	6 Nov. 1843	AMOUNT OF BOND:	$2,000
SECURITY:	John H. Coleman	PAGE:	549

. . . .

ORPHAN:	Edward S. Mason		
PARENT:	Valentine M. Mason	GUARDIAN:	John H. Nicholas
DATE:	6 Nov. 1843	AMOUNT OF BOND:	$1,000
SECURITY:	John H. Coleman	PAGE:	551

II, pages 553 thru 557

ORPHAN:	Sarah Thacker		
PARENT:	Isham Thacker	**GUARDIAN:**	Benjamin Thacker
DATE:	6 Nov. 1843	**AMOUNT OF BOND:**	$100
SECURITY:	Robert Wheeler	**PAGE:**	553

. . . .

ORPHAN:	Elizabeth Woodson		
PARENT:	Stephen Woodson	**GUARDIAN:**	John Norborne Morrison
DATE:	6 Nov. 1843	**AMOUNT OF BOND:**	$3,000
SECURITY:	Zachariah Lewis, Jr.	**PAGE:**	554

. . . .

ORPHAN:	Charles J., & Mary M. Meriwether		
PARENT:	Francis Meriwether	**GUARDIAN:**	Frank K. Nelson
DATE:	4 Dec. 1843	**AMOUNT OF BOND:**	$12,000
SECURITY:	Thomas W. Meriwether	**PAGE:**	555

. . . .

ORPHAN:	Jane A. Darrow		
PARENT:	Ludowick Darrow	**GUARDIAN:**	Henry A. Darrow
DATE:	6 May 1844	**AMOUNT OF BOND:**	$100
SECURITY:	Samuel W. Martin	**PAGE:**	556

. . . .

ORPHAN:	Elizabeth M., Lewis L., Caroline M., & Emily A. J. Poates		
PARENT:	Lewis L. Poates	**GUARDIAN:**	John L. Poates
DATE:	3 June 1844	**AMOUNT OF BOND:**	$2,500
SECURITY:	[none]	**PAGE:**	557

II, pages 558 thru 563

ORPHAN: John T. Magruder
PARENT: Allen B. Magruder GUARDIAN: [father] Allen B. Magruder
DATE: 1 July 1844 AMOUNT OF BOND: $1,200
SECURITY: John Timberlake PAGE: 558

. . . .

ORPHAN: Rachel C. Warwick
PARENT: Andrew S. Warwick GUARDIAN: William Woods
DATE: 1 July 1844 AMOUNT OF BOND: $1,000
SECURITY: George M. Woods PAGE: 559

. . . .

ORPHAN: Sarah W., & Phillip A. Darnielle, and Jenetta A. Beard
PARENT: John Darnielle GUARDIAN: Austin M. Appling
DATE: 5 Aug. 1844 AMOUNT OF BOND: $5,000
SECURITY: John H. Coleman PAGE: 561

. . . .

ORPHAN: Elizabeth R. Scott [over 14 years of age]
PARENT: John Scott GUARDIAN: William Wertenbaker
DATE: 5 Aug. 1844 AMOUNT OF BOND: $1,000
SECURITY: James A. Leitch PAGE: 563

. . . .

ORPHAN:
PARENT: GUARDIAN:
DATE: AMOUNT OF BOND:
SECURITY: PAGE:

SECTION III

BOND BOOK

1844 - 1852

III, pages 1 thru 9

ORPHAN: Celia A., Sam¹ M., Gasway B., & Chs C. Dyer
PARENT: Francis B. Dyer   GUARDIAN: Sally G. Dyer
DATE: 2 Sept. 1844   AMOUNT OF BOND: $1,000
SECURITY: John B. Hart   PAGE: 1

. . . .

ORPHAN: Franklin, Jeramy, Bernard, & Brightberry Fretwell
PARENT: Hudson Fretwell   GUARDIAN: Elizabeth Fretwell
DATE: 2 Sept. 1844   AMOUNT OF BOND: $10,000
SECURITY: Nath¹ Burnley   PAGE: 3
           Seth Burnley

. . . .

ORPHAN: Cynthia Ann Gardner
PARENT: Wilson Gardner   GUARDIAN: Bentley B. Ellis
DATE: 5 Nov. 1844   AMOUNT OF BOND: $100
SECURITY: Garland T. Brown   PAGE: 5

. . . .

ORPHAN: Joseph A., James H., Richard D., & Mary Jane Grinstead
PARENT: Js H. Grinstead   GUARDIAN: Thomas C. Bowen
DATE: 3 Feb. 1845   AMOUNT OF BOND: $6,000
SECURITY: William Smith   PAGE: 7
           Jechonias Yancey

. . . .

ORPHAN: Mildred L. Wood
PARENT: Thomas Wood   GUARDIAN: Alfred C. Wood
DATE: 3 Feb. 1845   AMOUNT OF BOND: $4,000
SECURITY: James B. Rogers   PAGE: 9

III, pages 11 thru 19

ORPHAN: Thomas Jones
PARENT: James Jones
GUARDIAN: Alexander Pope Abell
DATE: 3 March 1845
AMOUNT OF BOND: $1,200
SECURITY: John H. Bibb
PAGE: 11

. . . .

ORPHAN: George W., Isaac N., Mary Frances, & Sarah Jane Wood
PARENT: Jesse Wood
GUARDIAN: Bezaleel Brown
DATE: 7 April 1845
AMOUNT OF BOND: $800
SECURITY: Charles Brown
PAGE: 13

. . . .

ORPHAN: Thomas Addis, & Jane Louisa Emmett
PARENT: John P. Emmett
GUARDIAN: Mary Bird Emmett
DATE: 3 June 1845
AMOUNT OF BOND: $7,000
SECURITY: George Tucker
PAGE: 15

. . . .

ORPHAN: Warner Wood
PARENT: Robert W. Wood
GUARDIAN: James B. Rogers
DATE: 4 Aug. 1845
AMOUNT OF BOND: $6,000
SECURITY: James E. Chapman
PAGE: 17

. . . .

ORPHAN: Thomas Jones
PARENT: James W. Jones
GUARDIAN: James O. Hawley
DATE: 1 Sept. 1845
AMOUNT OF BOND: $1,100
SECURITY: Lewis B. Burnley[?]
PAGE: 19

III, pages 22 thru 30

ORPHAN: Joshua Smith
PARENT: William Smith   GUARDIAN: Leonard Drumheller
DATE: 1 Sept. 1845   AMOUNT OF BOND: $300
SECURITY: David Tinden   PAGE: 22

. . . .

ORPHAN: Charles G. Brown
PARENT: John Brown   GUARDIAN: Henry C. Moore
DATE: 6 Oct. 1845   AMOUNT OF BOND: $6,000
SECURITY: John Brown   PAGE: 24

. . . .

ORPHAN: Martha E., & Marietta Brown
PARENT: John Brown   GUARDIAN: John M. Carr
DATE: 6 Oct. 1845   AMOUNT OF BOND: $6,000
SECURITY: Joseph F. Wingfield, PAGE: 26
James W. Suddarth, James J. Jones,
George W. Craven

. . . .

ORPHAN: Frances V. Carnahan
PARENT: John W. Carnahan   GUARDIAN: Milner Woodson
DATE: 6 Oct. 1845   AMOUNT OF BOND: $80
SECURITY: Edwin Woodson   PAGE: 28
          Elisha C. Browning

. . . .

ORPHAN: James M. Mason
PARENT: Valentine M. Mason   GUARDIAN: Wilson C. Nicholas
DATE: 6 Oct. 1845   AMOUNT OF BOND: $2,500
SECURITY: John Morris   PAGE: 30

III, pages 32 thru 40

ORPHAN:	Thomas Rothwell		
PARENT:	Anderson Rothwell	GUARDIAN:	Hugh Foster
DATE:	6 Oct. 1845	AMOUNT OF BOND:	$700
SECURITY:	Wm. H. Browning Wm. M. Foster	PAGE:	32

. . . .

ORPHAN:	Melinda C. Thurmond		
PARENT:	Elisha H. Thurmond	GUARDIAN:	William P. Farish
DATE:	6 Oct. 1845	AMOUNT OF BOND:	$1,000
SECURITY:	John S. Cocke	PAGE:	34

. . . .

ORPHAN:	Letitia A. Goodman		
PARENT:	Nathan C. Goodman	GUARDIAN:	[mother] Sarah W. Goodman
DATE:	4 Nov. 1845	AMOUNT OF BOND:	$5,000
SECURITY:	David R. Goodman Walker Timberlake	PAGE:	36

. . . .

ORPHAN:	Reuben Lindsay		
PARENT:	Reuben Lindsay	GUARDIAN:	Stephen F. Sampson
DATE:	4 Nov. 1845	AMOUNT OF BOND:	$8,000
SECURITY:	James Lindsay George W. Craven	PAGE:	38

. . . .

ORPHAN:	Charlotte, & Lorna Moon		
PARENT:	Jacob Moon	GUARDIAN:	Thomas N. Trice
DATE:	4 Nov. 1845	AMOUNT OF BOND:	$12,000
SECURITY:	Anderson Trice	PAGE:	40

III, pages 42 thru 50

ORPHAN: Charles H., Robert A., Sally A., Billy P., & Daniel Price

PARENT: Stephen C. Price   GUARDIAN: Merewether L. Anderson

DATE: 3 Nov. 1845   AMOUNT OF BOND: $20,000

SECURITY: Benjn Wood,   PAGE: 42
Gabriel S. Harper, Thos. F. Lewis

. . . .

ORPHAN: Elizabeth Ann Pleasants

PARENT: Harriet Pleasants   GUARDIAN: Japhet Battles

DATE: 3 Nov. 1845   AMOUNT OF BOND: $800

SECURITY: Thomas Farrar   PAGE: 44

. . . .

ORPHAN: Pocahontas B., & Mary David Scott

PARENT: John Scott   GUARDIAN: William Wertenbaker

DATE: 4 Nov. 1845   AMOUNT OF BOND: $2,000

SECURITY: John Timberlake   PAGE: 46

. . . .

ORPHAN: Lavinia, James H., John, Charles, & George Wallace

PARENT: Michael Wallace   GUARDIAN: Lavinia Wallace

DATE: 3 Nov. 1845   AMOUNT OF BOND: $10,000

SECURITY: Lavinia Wallace   PAGE: 48

. . . .

ORPHAN: Sarah M. Woods

PARENT: John Woods   GUARDIAN: George W. Harris

DATE: 3 Nov. 1845   AMOUNT OF BOND: $40,000

SECURITY: Danl E. Watson   PAGE: 50
Jesse L. Heiskell

III, pages 52 thru 60

ORPHAN:	Sally W. Carr		
PARENT:	Samuel Carr	GUARDIAN:	William S. Dabney
DATE:	1 Dec. 1845	AMOUNT OF BOND:	$10,000
SECURITY:	Wm. W. Minor	PAGE:	52

· ·

ORPHAN: Carter H., William M., Mary E., & Martha J. Railey

PARENT: John M. Railey GUARDIAN: James A. Watson

DATE: 6 Jan. 1846 AMOUNT OF BOND: $12,000

SECURITY: Anderson Brown, Rice G. Barksdale, James M. Johnston, Thomas R. Bailey, Edwin H. Gooch   PAGE: 54

· ·

ORPHAN: Mary L., Wilhelmina M., Ellen F., and Adeline Bowen

PARENT: William Bowen GUARDIAN: [father] William Bowen

DATE: 6 April 1846 AMOUNT OF BOND: $300

SECURITY: Boswell P. Yates PAGE: 56

· ·

ORPHAN: William M. Morris

PARENT: William Morris GUARDIAN: Marcus Durrett

DATE: 6 April 1846 AMOUNT OF BOND: $20,000

SECURITY: Henry C. Moore, Stevens D. Hopkins, Wm. D. Hart, Jno. D. Moon, Jr., Richard M. Durrett   PAGE: 58

· ·

ORPHAN: Mary Pilson Wallace

PARENT: John Wallace GUARDIAN: William Smith

DATE: 4 May 1846 AMOUNT OF BOND: $4,000

SECURITY: John T. Antrim, Saml. O. Moon   PAGE: 60

III, pages 62 thru 70

ORPHAN:	Sally H., & William R. Burnley
PARENT:	William R. Burnley GUARDIAN: Nathaniel Burnley
DATE:	3 June 1846 AMOUNT OF BOND: $4,000
SECURITY:	Garland A. Garth PAGE: 62
	Thomas Wood

. . . .

ORPHAN:	Nancy Parish
PARENT:	Samuel Parish GUARDIAN: James S. Crewdson
DATE:	6 July 1846 AMOUNT OF BOND: $200
SECURITY:	Hudson Burton[?] PAGE: 64

. . . .

ORPHAN:	Charles L. Wingfield
PARENT:	Joseph Wingfield GUARDIAN: John J. Wingfield
DATE:	6 July 1846 AMOUNT OF BOND: $1,200
SECURITY:	Thomas Wingfield PAGE: 66

. . . .

ORPHAN:	Columbia A., Claudius E., & Eugene Norris
PARENT:	Thomas C. Norris GUARDIAN: Elizabeth Ann Norris
DATE:	3 Aug. 1846 AMOUNT OF BOND: $3,500
SECURITY:	Samuel Norris PAGE: 68

. . . .

ORPHAN:	James H. Norris
PARENT:	Thomas C. Norris GUARDIAN: James Woods
DATE:	3 Aug. 1846 AMOUNT OF BOND: $1,000
SECURITY:	William Smith PAGE: 70

III, pages 72 thru 80

ORPHAN: Thomas A. Norris
PARENT: Thomas C. Norris   GUARDIAN: Thomas R. Dunn
DATE: 3 Aug. 1846   AMOUNT OF BOND: $1,000
SECURITY: James E. Chapman   PAGE: 72

. . . .

ORPHAN: John G. Wallace
PARENT: John Wallace   GUARDIAN: William Smith
DATE: 3 Aug. 1846   AMOUNT OF BOND: $4,000
SECURITY: James Woods   PAGE: 74
Philip Edge

. . . .

ORPHAN: William F. N., & Martha M. N. Lobban
PARENT: James Lobban   GUARDIAN: [father] James Lobban
DATE: 7 Dec. 1846   AMOUNT OF BOND: $10,000
SECURITY: Peter McGehee   PAGE: 76
Drury Wood

. . . .

ORPHAN: Silas Hauss
PARENT: Daniel M. Haws   GUARDIAN: John Chewning
DATE: 5 July 1847   AMOUNT OF BOND: $100
SECURITY: Horatio J. Magruder   PAGE: 78

. . . .

ORPHAN: Frances Michie
PARENT: John J. Michie   GUARDIAN: James Michie
DATE: 1 Feb. 1847   AMOUNT OF BOND: $1,000
SECURITY: Wm. Garth   PAGE: 80

III, pages 82 thru 90

ORPHAN:	Ha [?] W., & William W. Reinhart		
PARENT:	E. W. Reinhart	GUARDIAN:	Catharine H. Reinhart
DATE:	1 Feb. 1847	AMOUNT OF BOND:	$1,200
SECURITY:	Wm. W. Minor	PAGE:	82

. . . .

ORPHAN:	Benjamin W., Thomas L., & Theodore L. Thurmond		
PARENT:	Elisha H. Thurmond	GUARDIAN:	Mary D. Thurmond
DATE:	1 Feb. 1847	AMOUNT OF BOND:	$2,500
SECURITY:	Wiley Dickenson Wm. C. Thurmond	PAGE:	84

. . . .

ORPHAN:	John N. C., & Catharine Stockton		
PARENT:	John N. C. Stockton	GUARDIAN:	George W. Randolph
DATE:	1 March 1847	AMOUNT OF BOND:	$40,000
SECURITY:	Thomas J. Randolph Benjamin F. Randolph	PAGE:	86

. . . .

ORPHAN:	Frances A. Michie		
PARENT:	John J. Michie	GUARDIAN:	James Michie
DATE:	5 April 1847	AMOUNT OF BOND:	$600
SECURITY:	William Garth	PAGE:	88

. . . .

ORPHAN:	Catharine F., Cornelia E. Michie		
PARENT:	James Michie, Jr.	GUARDIAN:	Octavius G. Michie
DATE:	6 April 1847	AMOUNT OF BOND:	$15,000
SECURITY:	James B. Rogers Theodore A. Michie	PAGE:	90

III, pages 92 thru 100

ORPHAN: Joseph P., Lucian A., Orvin, & Eugene O. Michie
PARENT: James Michie, Jr.   GUARDIAN: William T. Early
DATE: 6 April 1847   AMOUNT OF BOND: $30,000
SECURITY: James Michie   PAGE: 92

. . . .

ORPHAN: Virginia Anne Michie
PARENT: James Michie, Jr.   GUARDIAN: Octavius G. Michie
DATE: 6 April 1847   AMOUNT OF BOND: $7,000
SECURITY: Frances A. Michie   PAGE: 94

. . . .

ORPHAN: Ann E. Bruce
PARENT: Nancy Bruce   GUARDIAN: Nelson Barksdale
DATE: 7 June 1847   AMOUNT OF BOND: $3,000
SECURITY: J. J. Bowcock   PAGE: 96
          John B. Doughy[?]
Note from E. W. Bruce states that Ann E. Bruce is his granddaughter
. . . .

ORPHAN: Sarah E. Woods
PARENT: William Woods   GUARDIAN: [father] William Woods
DATE: 7 June 1847   AMOUNT OF BOND: $1,000
SECURITY: John Jones   PAGE: 98

. . . .

ORPHAN: Elizabeth McDaniel
PARENT: [an illegitimate child]   GUARDIAN: Andrew W. Gibson
DATE: 4 Aug. 1847   AMOUNT OF BOND: $100
SECURITY: John Gibson   PAGE: 100

III, pages 102 thru 110

ORPHAN:	Robert A. Price		
PARENT:	Stephen C. Price	GUARDIAN:	Merewether L. Anderson
DATE:	2 Aug. 1847	AMOUNT OF BOND:	$10,000
SECURITY:	Thomas F. Lewis Gabriel S. Harper	PAGE:	102

. . . .

ORPHAN:	Lavinia Ann Chisholm		
PARENT:	Menucan[?] Chisholm	GUARDIAN:	William Chisholm
DATE:	4 Oct. 1847	AMOUNT OF BOND:	$600
SECURITY:	George C. Gilmer	PAGE:	104

. . . .

ORPHAN:	Sally, Lucy, John, James, Spotswood, Thomas H., & Mary Goodloe		
PARENT:	John H. Goodloe	GUARDIAN:	Addison M. Goodloe
DATE:	4 Oct. 1847	AMOUNT OF BOND:	$100
SECURITY:	Bozwell P. Yates	PAGE:	106

. . . .

ORPHAN:	Thomas L. Rogers		
PARENT:	Parmenas Rogers	GUARDIAN:	Giles B. Rogers
DATE:	4 Oct. 1847	AMOUNT OF BOND:	$600
SECURITY:	James B. Rogers	PAGE:	108

. . . .

ORPHAN:	Martha J. Woods		
PARENT:	George W. Woods	GUARDIAN:	[Col?] William Woods
DATE:	6 Dec. 1847	AMOUNT OF BOND:	$8,000
SECURITY:	William A. Woods Andrew M. Woods	PAGE:	110

III, pages 112 thru 120

ORPHAN: Jacob Warwick Woods
PARENT: George M. Woods GUARDIAN: Wm. Woods
DATE: 6 Dec. 1847 AMOUNT OF BOND: $8,000
SECURITY: Peter McGehee PAGE: 112

. . . .

ORPHAN: Mary E. Woods
PARENT: George M. Woods GUARDIAN: Wm. A. Woods
DATE: 6 Dec. 1847 AMOUNT OF BOND: $8,000
SECURITY: Wm. Woods PAGE: 114
Andrew M. Woods

. . . .

ORPHAN: Albert W. Gantt
PARENT: Henry Gantt GUARDIAN: Benjamin M. Perkins
DATE: 3 Jan. 1848 AMOUNT OF BOND: $16,000
SECURITY: Robert L. Jefferson PAGE: 116

. . . .

ORPHAN: Martha A., Emma A., Mary E., Harriet A., Richard, & Joseph
PARENT: Richard Mathews GUARDIAN: Harriet Mathews
DATE: 7 Feb. 1848 AMOUNT OF BOND: $25,000
SECURITY: John Dundoe[?] PAGE: 118

. . . .

ORPHAN: John, & William Mathews
PARENT: Richard Mathews GUARDIAN: Harriet Mathews
DATE: 7 Feb. 1848 AMOUNT OF BOND: $25,000
SECURITY: John Dundoe[?] PAGE: 120

III, pages 122 thru 130

ORPHAN:	Eliza E. Priddy		
PARENT:	John Priddy	GUARDIAN:	James Vermillion
DATE:	7 Feb. 1848	AMOUNT OF BOND:	$100
SECURITY:	William W. Via	PAGE:	122

. . . .

ORPHAN:	Jeremiah, & Joshua Sutton		
PARENT:	Wisdom Sutton	GUARDIAN:	David Watts
DATE:	6 March 1848	AMOUNT OF BOND:	$2,000
SECURITY:	Wm. Crenshaw	PAGE:	124

. . . .

ORPHAN:	William Lee		
PARENT:	John Lee	GUARDIAN:	James A. Leitch
DATE:	6 March 1848	AMOUNT OF BOND:	$50
SECURITY:	Drury Wood	PAGE:	126

. . . .

ORPHAN:	John R. Hall		
PARENT:	John Hall	GUARDIAN:	Lucy R. R. Hall
DATE:	3 April 1848	AMOUNT OF BOND:	$400
SECURITY:	Bluford Marshall	PAGE:	128

. . . .

ORPHAN:	Sarah J. Alexander		
PARENT:	Andrew Alexander	GUARDIAN:	Tyree Dollins
DATE:	1 May 1848	AMOUNT OF BOND:	$3,000
SECURITY:	James G. Alexander Hudson Oaks	PAGE:	130

III, pages 132 thru 140

ORPHAN: James L., Virginia H., Euphemia H., Sandy H., George W., & Sarah L. Craven
PARENT: William L. Craven GUARDIAN: [father] William L. Crave
DATE: 4 Sept. 1848 AMOUNT OF BOND: $2,700
SECURITY: Stapleton C. Sneed PAGE: 132

. . . .

ORPHAN: Elizabeth Fisher
PARENT: Robert Fisher GUARDIAN: George B. Brown
DATE: 4 Sept. 1848 AMOUNT OF BOND: $300
SECURITY: J. Augustus Brown PAGE: 134

. . . .

ORPHAN: Sarah E., Zachariah L., & George W. Gilmer
PARENT: George C. Gilmer GUARDIAN: [father] George C. Gi
DATE: 4 Sept. 1848 AMOUNT OF BOND: $300
SECURITY: James A. Morris PAGE: 136

. . . .

ORPHAN: George N., Robert W., Elizabeth D., Alice L., & Ellen O. Lewis
PARENT: Robert W. Lewis GUARDIAN: [father] Robert W. Lewis
DATE: 4 Sept. 1848 AMOUNT OF BOND: $2,500
SECURITY: Merewether L. Anderson PAGE: 138

. . . .

ORPHAN: Stapleton Emmett Sneed
PARENT: Stapleton C. Sneed GUARDIAN: [father] Stapleton C. Snee
DATE: 4 Sept. 1848 AMOUNT OF BOND: $500
SECURITY: Wm. L. Craven PAGE: 140

III, pages 142 thru 148

ORPHAN: Marietta Brown

PARENT: John Brown GUARDIAN: William A. Brown

DATE: 6 Nov. 1848 AMOUNT OF BOND: $6,000

SECURITY: Henry C. Moore, Boswill P. Yates, Jerome B. Wood PAGE: 142

. . . .

ORPHAN: Charles B., James H., & William T. Carter

PARENT: Burnet Carter GUARDIAN: James F. Burnley

DATE: 6 Nov. 1848 AMOUNT OF BOND: $300

SECURITY: Stokes Tunstill PAGE: 144

. . . .

ORPHAN: Iscietta[?] L. Hudson

PARENT: Charles Hudson GUARDIAN: Zachariah R. Lewis

DATE: 6 Nov. 1848 AMOUNT OF BOND: $30,000

SECURITY: Daniel P. Lewis PAGE: 146

. . . .

ORPHAN: Richard, Edward A., & Henry R. Pollard

PARENT: Richard Pollard GUARDIAN: [father] Richard Pollard

DATE: 6 Nov. 1848 AMOUNT OF BOND: $7,000

SECURITY: Margaret C. Henderson, Virginia Pollard, James R. Pollard, Lucy E. Pollard PAGE: 148

   On page 147 are statements from Richard Pollard's adult children, Margaret C. Henderson, Virginia Pollard, James R. Pollard, and Lucy E. Pollard, indicating their willingness to furnish security for their father who wishes to qualify as statutory guardian of his minor children, Richard, Edward A., and Henry R. Margaret C. Henderson indicates that she has an interest in the Blue[?] Park estate, as widow of the late James P. Henderson, as well as sharing an interest in the Alta Vista estate with her siblings. On page 147 Richard Pollard also itemized the contents of the $18,000 estate bequeathed to his children by the late Robert Rives.

III, pages 150 thru 158

ORPHAN: Mary S., Virginia A., & John H. Crawford
PARENT: Malcom F. Crawford   GUARDIAN: [father] Malcom F. Crawford
DATE: 4 Dec. 1848   AMOUNT OF BOND: $1,500
SECURITY: George W. Craven   PAGE: 150

. . . .

ORPHAN: Peter H., & Jesse L. Craven
PARENT: George W. Craven   GUARDIAN: [father] George W. Craven
DATE: 4 Dec. 1848   AMOUNT OF BOND: $1,000
SECURITY: James Alexander   PAGE: 152
Malcom F. Crawford

. . . .

ORPHAN: Mary R. Craven
PARENT: John D. Craven   GUARDIAN: James Alexander
[not deceased]
DATE: 4 Dec. 1848   AMOUNT OF BOND: $500
SECURITY: George W. Craven   PAGE: 154
Malcom F. Crawford

. . . .

ORPHAN: Andrew J., Edmund J., Maria L., & Susan C. Craven
PARENT: John D. Craven   GUARDIAN: George W. Craven
[not deceased]
DATE: 4 Dec. 1848   AMOUNT OF BOND: $2,000
SECURITY: James Alexander   PAGE: 156
Malcom F. Crawford

. . . .

ORPHAN: Susan C., James D., & Walter G. Garth
PARENT: Garland A. Garth   GUARDIAN: [father] Garland A. Garth
DATE: 4 Dec. 1848   AMOUNT OF BOND: $100
SECURITY: James W. Saunders   PAGE: 158

III, pages 160 thru 168

ORPHAN: Sarah M. Phelps

PARENT: Charles Phelps GUARDIAN: James W. Drumheller

DATE: 4 Dec. 1848 AMOUNT OF BOND: $1,000

SECURITY: William A. Brown, PAGE: 160
James W. Lyon, Benjamin H. Eubank,
Hudson Strange

. . . .

ORPHAN: John A. G., James M. M., & Ann M. Davis

PARENT: Eugene Davis GUARDIAN: [father] Eugene Davis

DATE: 2 Jan. 1849 AMOUNT OF BOND: $30,000

SECURITY: Ann C. Morris PAGE: 162

. . . .

ORPHAN: Susan C., James D., & Walter G. Garth

PARENT: Garland A. Garth GUARDIAN: [father] Garland A. Garth

DATE: 5 Feb. 1849 AMOUNT OF BOND: $4,000

SECURITY: Garland Garth PAGE: 164

. . . .

ORPHAN: Martha B. Mosby

PARENT: Benjamin Mosby GUARDIAN: Hezekiah Mosby

DATE: 6 March 1849 AMOUNT OF BOND: $10,000

SECURITY: William P. Farish PAGE: 166
John Mosby

. . . .

ORPHAN: Joseph, & Jane Lewis Perkins

PARENT: Daniel H. Perkins GUARDIAN: Benjamin Wood

DATE: 2 April 1849 AMOUNT OF BOND: $4,000

SECURITY: John Wood, Jr. PAGE: 168
M. L. Anderson

III, pages 170 thru 176

ORPHAN: Emma J. Craven

PARENT: John D. Craven [not deceased]

GUARDIAN: George W. Craven

DATE: 7 May 1849

AMOUNT OF BOND: $500

SECURITY: James Alexander
William L. Craven

PAGE: 170

. . . .

ORPHAN: Evalina and Sallie T. Norris [over 14 years of age]; and Opie Norris [under 14 years of age]

PARENT: Opie Norris

GUARDIAN: Alexander Rives

DATE: 6 May 1850

AMOUNT OF BOND: $40,000

SECURITY: George Rives

PAGE: 172

. . . .

ORPHAN: Opie Norris Watson [under 14 years of age]

PARENT: Matthew P. Watson

GUARDIAN: Alexander Rives

DATE: 6 May 1850

AMOUNT OF BOND: $40,000

SECURITY: George Rives

PAGE: 172

The bond states that Opie Norris Watson is also interested in the estate of Opie Norris, deceased.

. . . .

ORPHAN: John W., Daniel W., George B., Henry P., Susan F., Mary E., & Amanda M. Marshall

PARENT: Epphroditus Marshall [not deceased]

GUARDIAN: James Marshall

DATE: 4 June 1849

AMOUNT OF BOND: $1,000

SECURITY: Alexander Rives

PAGE: 174

. . . .

ORPHAN: Samuel, George Wm., Flourance, & Isaac Crawford

PARENT: James W. Crawford

GUARDIAN: [father] James W. Crawford

DATE: 2 July 1849

AMOUNT OF BOND: $1,500

SECURITY: James Blackwell, Richard D. Simms, James Simms

PAGE: 176

III, pages 178 thru 186

ORPHAN: Richard D. Simms, Jr., & Julia H. Simms [both over 14 years old]
PARENT: Isaac Simms   GUARDIAN: [uncle] Richard D. Simms
DATE: 2 July 1849   AMOUNT OF BOND: $3,000
SECURITY: James W. Crawford   PAGE: 178
           James Simms

. . . .

ORPHAN: George M. Hord
PARENT: Lewis Hord   GUARDIAN: [father] Lewis Hord
DATE: 7 Aug. 1849   AMOUNT OF BOND: $1,000
SECURITY: George H. Crank   PAGE: 180

. . . .

ORPHAN: Mary Frances Grayson
PARENT: Joseph Grayson   GUARDIAN: William D. Grayson
DATE: 1 Oct. 1849   AMOUNT OF BOND: $3,000
SECURITY: Thomas H. Grayson   PAGE: 182
           John Grayson

. . . .

ORPHAN: Henry, Sarah, Jane, & John Gentry
PARENT: Pascal B. Gentry   GUARDIAN: James M. Dunn
           [not deceased]
DATE: 3 Dec. 1849   AMOUNT OF BOND: $1,700
SECURITY: Gabriel Maupin   PAGE: 184

. . . .

ORPHAN: Edwin S. Crawford
PARENT: M. F. Crawford   GUARDIAN: George W. Craven
           [not deceased]
DATE: 8 Jan. 1850   AMOUNT OF BOND: $500
SECURITY: William L. Craven   PAGE: 186

III, pages 188 thru 196

ORPHAN:	Martha J. Woods [over 14 years of age]		
PARENT:	George M. Woods	GUARDIAN:	[brother] William A. Woods
DATE:	8 Jan. 1850	AMOUNT OF BOND:	$6,000
SECURITY:	George M. Woods Andrew N. Woods	PAGE:	188

Note indicates former guardian, Col. Wm. Woods, had died by Jan. 1850

. . . .

ORPHAN:	Alexander, George W., & John B. Garrett		
PARENT:	John B. Garrett	GUARDIAN:	[father] John B. Garrett
DATE:	4 Feb. 1850	AMOUNT OF BOND:	$5,000
SECURITY:	Thomas J. Randolph	PAGE:	190

. . . .

ORPHAN:	John M., Lucy Ann., Clifton R., William D., & Chapman M. Wood		
PARENT:	William T. Wood	GUARDIAN:	[father] William T. Wood
DATE:	4 March 1850	AMOUNT OF BOND:	$300
SECURITY:	Thomas M. Via	PAGE:	192

Note indicates that these infants mother was formerly Martha Maupin, d
and that she held an interest in the estate of Thomas Maupin, decd.

. . . .

ORPHAN:	Rutha Wood		
PARENT:	Achilles Wood	GUARDIAN:	Samuel Wood
DATE:	4 March 1850	AMOUNT OF BOND:	$2,000
SECURITY:	William T. Early James B. Rogers	PAGE:	194

. . . .

ORPHAN:	Susan C., James D., & Walter G. Garth		
PARENT:	Garland A. Garth	GUARDIAN:	[father] Garland A. Garth
DATE:	6 Aug. 1850	AMOUNT OF BOND:	$1,200
SECURITY:	Drury W. Burnley	PAGE:	196

III, pages 198 thru 206

ORPHAN: Martha A. [age 15], Franklin B. [age 17], & Fontaine [age 14] Richards
PARENT: Fontaine Richards GUARDIAN: John S. Richards
DATE: 7 Oct. 1850 AMOUNT OF BOND: $2,600
SECURITY: George W. Richards, Joseph R. Richards, David W. Mills PAGE: 198

. . . .

ORPHAN: Thornton, & Susan J. Baxter
PARENT: Joseph F. Baxter GUARDIAN: Susan E. Baxter
DATE: 4 Nov. 1850 AMOUNT OF BOND: $8,000
SECURITY: Keating S. Nelson PAGE: 200

. . . .

ORPHAN: Julia Ann Thomas [over 14 years of age]
PARENT: Samuel Thomas GUARDIAN: J. J. Bowcock
DATE: 4 Nov. 1850 AMOUNT OF BOND: $500
SECURITY: Nelson Barksdale PAGE: 202

. . . .

ORPHAN: Thomas G. Michie
PARENT: James Michie GUARDIAN: William T. Early
DATE: 2 Dec. 1850 AMOUNT OF BOND: $20,000
SECURITY: John E. Michie, Alexander H. Michie PAGE: 204

. . . .

ORPHAN: Theresha, & Adiline Michie
PARENT: James Michie GUARDIAN: Augustus Michie
DATE: 2 Dec. 1850 AMOUNT OF BOND: $40,000
SECURITY: Wm. Michie, John E. Michie PAGE: 206

III, pages 208 thru 216

ORPHAN: Henry Clay Michie

PARENT: James Michie GUARDIAN: Susan F. Michie

DATE: 2 Dec. 1850 AMOUNT OF BOND: $20,000

SECURITY: William Garth PAGE: 208

. . . .

ORPHAN: James Jeffries

PARENT: Alfred K. Jeffries GUARDIAN: William Jeffries

DATE: 6 Jan. 1851 AMOUNT OF BOND: $1,600

SECURITY: David W. Jeffries PAGE: 210

. . . .

ORPHAN: Thomas B. Jones

PARENT: James W. Jones GUARDIAN: James O. Hawley

DATE: 6 Jan. 1851 AMOUNT OF BOND: $1,100

SECURITY: John Morrow PAGE: 212

James O. Hawley and John Morrow are citizens of the county of Lewis,
This bond was required by Henry Harris, Exor. of Lewis B. Bailey, dec
. . . .

ORPHAN: Lucian A., Orin, & Eugene O. Michie

PARENT: James Michie, Jr. GUARDIAN: William T. Early

DATE: 6 Jan. 1851 AMOUNT OF BOND: $20,000

SECURITY: James E. Chapman, PAGE: 214
Michael Catterton, Wm. Blackwell

. . . .

ORPHAN: Sarah M. Phelps

PARENT: Charles Phelps GUARDIAN: James W. Drumheller

DATE: 6 Jan. 1851 AMOUNT OF BOND: $1,000

SECURITY: Nathaniel Burnley PAGE: 216

III, pages 218 thru 228

ORPHAN:	Mary C. Turner [age 15 years]
PARENT:	William D. Turner GUARDIAN: Christopher L. Fowler
DATE:	6 Jan. 1851 AMOUNT OF BOND: $8,000
SECURITY:	William N. Ragland PAGE: 218

- -

ORPHAN:	William Emmet Coleman
PARENT:	Roderick S. Coleman GUARDIAN: St. George Tucker
DATE:	3 Feb. 1851 AMOUNT OF BOND: $200
SECURITY:	Richard T. W. Duke PAGE: 220
	Allan R. Magruder

- -

ORPHAN:	Ann Jones
PARENT:	Turner Jones GUARDIAN: John S. Saunders
DATE:	3 March 1851 AMOUNT OF BOND: $100
SECURITY:	Chiles M. Brand PAGE: 222

- -

ORPHAN:	Edward A., & Henry R. Pollard [over 14 years of age]
PARENT:	Richard Pollard GUARDIAN: James R. Pollard [brother]
DATE:	5 May 1851 AMOUNT OF BOND: $2,400
SECURITY:	Margaret C. Henderson PAGE: 224

- -

ORPHAN:	William W. McClung
PARENT:	William W. McClung GUARDIAN: Richard M. Durrett
DATE:	2 June 1851 AMOUNT OF BOND: $7,000
SECURITY:	Marcus Durrett PAGE: 228
	James Durrett

III, pages 230 thru 240

ORPHAN: James Norris

PARENT: Thomas C. Norris GUARDIAN: Samuel Wood

DATE: 2 April 1849 AMOUNT OF BOND: $1,500

SECURITY: Brightberry B. Garth PAGE: 230

. . . .

ORPHAN: Mary Jane Clarke [over 14 years of age] [a resident of the state of Alabama]

PARENT: Thomas and Elizabeth Clarke GUARDIAN: James W. Saunders

DATE: 4 Aug. 1851 AMOUNT OF BOND: $5,000

SECURITY: Drury W. Burnley
John J. Bowcock PAGE: 232

. . . .

ORPHAN: William D. Wood

PARENT: David Wood GUARDIAN: Julianna Wood [mother] [of Rockingham Co., Va.]

DATE: 4 Aug. 1851 AMOUNT OF BOND: $10,000

SECURITY: John Dundore PAGE: 234

. . . .

ORPHAN: George W. Carr

PARENT: Bernard Carr GUARDIAN: [mother] Nancy Carr

DATE: 1 Sept. 1851 AMOUNT OF BOND: $2,000

SECURITY: John M. Carr
Overton Carr PAGE: 238

. . . .

ORPHAN: Nancy W. Carr

PARENT: Bernard Carr GUARDIAN: [mother] Nancy Carr

DATE: 1 Sept. 1851 AMOUNT OF BOND: $2,000

SECURITY: John M. Carr
Overton Carr PAGE: 240

III, pages 244 thru 252

ORPHAN: Mary Rebecca Wingfield
PARENT: Thomas Wingfield   GUARDIAN: [father] Thomas Wingfield
DATE: 1 Sept. 1851   AMOUNT OF BOND: $50
SECURITY: Lewis Sowell   PAGE: 244

. . . .

ORPHAN: Susan C. Colston
PARENT: Thomas M. Colston   GUARDIAN: Raleigh Colston
DATE: 4 Nov. 1851   AMOUNT OF BOND: $20,000
SECURITY: Nannie F. Colston   PAGE: 246

. . . .

ORPHAN: Thomas A., Walter M., & Eliza A. Powell [all over 14 years old]
PARENT: Samuel Powell   GUARDIAN: Paul Tilman, Jr.
DATE: 3 Nov. 1851   AMOUNT OF BOND: $4,000
SECURITY: B. B. Garth,   PAGE: 248
John T. Wood, Wm. P. Jarman,
John Kidd

. . . .

ORPHAN: William C. Tinder
PARENT: Ephraim Tinder   GUARDIAN: Mary J. Tinder
DATE: 3 Nov. 1851   AMOUNT OF BOND: $600
SECURITY: Caleb S. Abell   PAGE: 250

. . . .

ORPHAN: Jane, & Margaret P. Dawson
PARENT: Nelson Dawson   GUARDIAN: William Graves
DATE: 1 Dec. 1851   AMOUNT OF BOND: $4,000
SECURITY: John B. Spiece   PAGE: 252
Albert H. Cleaveland

III, pages 254 thru 262

ORPHAN: Sarah Lane
PARENT: William Lane GUARDIAN: George W. Boothe
DATE: 6 Jan. 1852 AMOUNT OF BOND: $100
SECURITY: A. J. Shepherd PAGE: 254

. . . .

ORPHAN: Rebecca Seay
PARENT: William Seay GUARDIAN: William C. Gay
DATE: 5 Jan. 1852 AMOUNT OF BOND: $100
SECURITY: John George PAGE: 256

. . . .

ORPHAN: Susan A., Mary E., & Sarah C. Snow ["oldest about 9 years ol
PARENT: Reuben D. Snow GUARDIAN: James F. Burnley
[died in 1849]
DATE: 1 March 1852 AMOUNT OF BOND: $1,000
SECURITY: Nathaniel Burnley PAGE: 258

. . . .

ORPHAN: Arthelia E. Wheat ["now in her sixteenth year"]
PARENT: Elijah T. Wheat GUARDIAN: [uncle] Horatio T. Wheat
DATE: 1 March 1852 AMOUNT OF BOND: $1,200
SECURITY: Edward Coles PAGE: 260

. . . .

ORPHAN: Mary Ann Lama
PARENT: William Lama GUARDIAN: James C. Gentry
DATE: 5 April 1852 AMOUNT OF BOND: $100
SECURITY: George Slaughter PAGE: 262

III, pages 264 thru 272

ORPHAN: William A., & Benjamin F. Trice
PARENT: Benjamin F. Trice GUARDIAN: Owen C. Bransford
DATE: 5 April 1852 AMOUNT OF BOND: $2,000
SECURITY: William B. Phillips PAGE: 264

. . . .

ORPHAN: Lucy Ann Trice
PARENT: Benjamin F. Trice GUARDIAN: John Vowles
DATE: 5 April 1852 AMOUNT OF BOND: $1,000
SECURITY: William B. Phillips PAGE: 266

. . . .

ORPHAN: John D. Edwards ["a non resident"]
PARENT: Hiram G. Edwards GUARDIAN: [father] Hiram G. Edwards
DATE: 7 June 1852 AMOUNT OF BOND: $12,000
SECURITY: Elisha J. Williams, PAGE: 268
Benjamin Herndon, James P. Douglass,
Magil O. Douglass

. . . .

ORPHAN: Lewis, Frank, William, & Martha Garrison
PARENT: Ralph Garrison GUARDIAN: Ira Chapman Garrison
DATE: 7 June 1852 AMOUNT OF BOND: $400
SECURITY: Chiles M. Brand PAGE: 270

. . . .

ORPHAN: Charles Smith Maupin
PARENT: William A. Maupin GUARDIAN: Addison Maupin
DATE: 8 June 1852 AMOUNT OF BOND: $15,000
SECURITY: Chapman W. Maupin PAGE: 272

III, pages 274 thru 282

ORPHAN: Nancy E., Sandy, Barbara A., & John W. C. Gibson
PARENT: John Gibson   GUARDIAN: George J. Gibson
DATE: 2 Aug. 1852   AMOUNT OF BOND: $2,400
SECURITY: Richard Dossey   PAGE: 274

. . . .

ORPHAN: John Martin
PARENT: Benjamin Martin   GUARDIAN: Sarah Martin
DATE: 2 Aug. 1852   AMOUNT OF BOND: $1,200
SECURITY: Lindsay Woodson   PAGE: 276

. . . .

ORPHAN: John N. C., & Catharine Stockton [over 14 years of age]
PARENT: John N. C. Stockton GUARDIAN: William J. Robertson
DATE: 3 Aug. 1852   AMOUNT OF BOND: $40,000
SECURITY: William P. Farish, PAGE: 278
Thomas L. Farish, Thomas J. Cooke
Note indicates G. W. Randolph was formerly guardian of these childrn
. . . .

ORPHAN: Andrew J., Edmund J., Maria L., & Susan C. Craven
PARENT: John D. Craven   GUARDIAN: Nathaniel H. Massie
        [not deceased]
DATE: 7 Sept. 1852   AMOUNT OF BOND: $2,000
SECURITY: James Lobban   PAGE: 280

. . . .

ORPHAN: Mary M. Cloar
PARENT: GUARDIAN: Elisha M. Herndon
DATE: 4 Oct. 1852   AMOUNT OF BOND: $100
SECURITY: James William Points PAGE: 282

III, pages 284 thru 292

ORPHAN: Ann C. Fretwell

PARENT: William C. Fretwell   GUARDIAN: Vienna L. Fretwell

DATE: 4 Oct. 1852   AMOUNT OF BOND: $1,200

SECURITY: George W. Kinsolving, **PAGE:** 284
William G. Barksdale, Thomas C. Bowen

. . . .

ORPHAN: William S., Oscar W., Martha J., & Edgar Head

PARENT: Valentine Head   GUARDIAN: Lucy J. Head

DATE: 4 Oct. 1852   AMOUNT OF BOND: $15,000

SECURITY: George M. Kinsolving   PAGE: 286
Henry J. Clarke

. . . .

ORPHAN: Willis M. Head

PARENT: Valentine Head   GUARDIAN: Henry E. Head

DATE: 4 Oct. 1852   AMOUNT OF BOND: $4,000

SECURITY: George W. Kinsolving   PAGE: 288
Henry J. Clarke

. . . .

ORPHAN: Thomas, Walter M., & Eliza A. Powell

PARENT: Samuel Powell   GUARDIAN: Blan Rea

DATE: 4 Oct. 1852   AMOUNT OF BOND: $3,600

SECURITY: William H. Wayland   PAGE: 290
William Graves

. . . .

ORPHAN: Thomas B. Watts

PARENT: James D. Watts   GUARDIAN: David R. Goodman

DATE: 7 Dec. 1852   AMOUNT OF BOND: $1,500

SECURITY: Seth Burnley   PAGE: 292

INDEX

INDEX, page 1

Abell, Alexander Pope: III, 11
   Caleb: LB, 67
   Caleb S.: LB, 61, 67, 70, 77; II, 39, 161, 257, 347; III, 250
   John S.: LB, 67; II, 81, 177
   Joshua: LB, 61
   Joshua W.: LB, 67, 78; II, 143, 455
   Richard S.: II, 81, 161, 483
Alexander, Andrew: LB, 32; III, 130
   Hugh: LB, 1
   James: III, 152, 154, 156, 170
   James G.: III, 130
   John: LB, 32
   Joseph: II, 19
   Sarah J.: III, 130
   William: LB, 20
Allen, Catherine: LB, 9, 13
   Dorotha: LB, 9, 14
   Hancock: LB, 22
   Isaac: LB, 30
   James: LB, 30
   James D.: LB, 63, 69, 78
   Polly: LB, 9, 14
   Richard H.: LB, 9, 13, 14, 63, 69
Allfred, Eliza: II, 13
   James: II, 13
Ames, Eli: II, 321
   Elizabeth L.: II, 321
   Samuel B.: II, 321
Ammonet, Thomas: II, 29, 417
Anderson, Anne: II, 71
   Ann E.: LB, 64
   Catharine: II, 73
   David: LB, 20
   Edmund: LB, 5, 28, 36, 48, 64, 81
   Frances: II, 71
   James: II, 73
   Lucy M.: LB, 28
   M. L.: III, 168
   Martha: LB, 74
   Mary B.: LB, 74
   Merewether: III, 42
   Merewether L.: II, 469 [398]; III, 102, 138
   Nathaniel: LB, 41
   Nathaniel, Jr.: LB, 35
   Nathaniel, Sr.: LB, 35
   Overton: LB, 74, 81
   Overton C.: II, 93, 113, 115
   Robert: LB, 31
   Sarah T.: LB, 81
   William: LB, 74
   William Lewis: LB, 36
Angel, Thomas: II, 409
Antrim, John T.: III, 60
Appleberry, Frances: II, 529
   John: LB, 57, 63
   John James: II, 529
   Ludamon: II, 529
   Martha: LB, 63

Appleberry, Mary: LB, 57
  Rush: II, 529
  Selina: II, 529
  Virginia Ann: II, 529
  William: LB, 57
  William S.: II, 529
Appling, Austin M.: II, 561
Argyle, John W.: LB, 81
Atkins, Jesse: LB, 64
Atkinson, James: II, 279
Austin, Ann: LB, 72
  Betsy: LB, 32
  Cally: LB, 32, 72
  David: LB, 32, 72, 78
  Durrett: LB, 32, 72
  Elizabeth E.: II, 197, 501
  Fanny: LB, 32
  Francis L.: II, 197, 501
  Garrett: LB, 32, 72
  Henry: LB, 32, 72
  Henry O.: II, 197, 501
  John T.: II, 197, 501
  Lilbourn M.: II, 197
  Milly: LB, 32, 72
  Nancy: LB, 32
  Obediah: II, 197, 501
  Thomas: LB, 72, 78
  Walker: LB, 32, 72
  Willis: LB, 32
Baber, James: II, 199, 397
  Robert: II, 199, 397
  Thomas: II, 199, 397
Bailey, Albert: II, 305, 391
  Callum: LB, 6
  Charles C.: II, 391
  Charles F.: II, 305
  Charles M.: II, 385
  Fanny: LB, 6
  George W.: II, 305, 391
  Ira T.: II, 305, 391
  James: II, 123
  Jane: II, 123
  John: LB, 70, 305, 391
  John H.: II, 305, 391
  Lewis: II, 385
  Lewis B.: II, 535; III, 212
  Polly (Goodin): II, 305
  Rice: II, 205
  Thomas R.: II, 201, 507; III, 54
  Waller: II, 305, 391
  Wilson: LB, 74
Ballard, Austin: LB, 78
  Bland: LB, 44, 59
  Bennett D.: LB, 44
  Burnett D.: LB, 59
  Edward: LB, 39
  Garland: LB, 44, 59

Ballard, George: LB, 39
  John: LB, 39
  Thomas: LB, 22, II, 509
  Wilson: LB, 78
Bankhead, Charles L.: II, 133, 139, 141, 259
  Charles Lewis: II, 133
  John: II, 141
  John, Sr.: II, 141
  Mary Jane: II, 132
  Thomas M. R.: II, 141, 259
  William: II, 141
  William S.: II, 139
Barclay [or Barkley]
  Anna M.: LB, 62
  Jane Turner: LB, 62
  Mary C.: LB, 68
  Mary Elizabeth: LB, 62
  Robert: LB, 62, 68
  Thomas: LB, 62
Barker, Polly: LB, 6
Barkley, see Barclay
Barksdale, Goodman: LB, 20, 27, 62
  John H.: LB, 31; II, 501
  Jonathan: LB, 27, 31
  Nelson: LB, 10, 18, 31, 59; II, 19, 149, 329, 331; III, 96, 202
  Rice G.: III, 54
  Samuel: LB, 10, 18, 62
  Samuel C.: LB, 73
  William: LB, 31
  William G.: II, 427; III, 284
Barnett, Judy: II, 21
  Mary: II, 21
  Nathan J.: II, 321
Battles, Japhet: III, 44
Baxter, Joseph F.: III, 200
  Susan E.: III, 200
  Susan J.: III, 200
  Thornton: III, 200
Beard, Jenetta A.: II, 561
Beck, Andrew: LB, 7; II, 183
  Jane: LB, 7
  Joseph: LB, 7
  Mildred: II, 181
  Reuben: II, 181, 183
  Reuben M.: II, 183
  William: II, 181
Becks, Lucinda: LB, 72
  Lucy: LB, 72
  Thomas: LB, 72
Beddow, Thomas: LB, 71
Bell, James: LB, 9, 12
  Sally Jefferson: LB, 19
  Thomas: LB, 19
Bernard, Joseph: LB, 39; II, 55
  Lucy Jane: II, 55
Berry, George: LB, 9, 14
  Rebbecca: LB, 9, 14
Bibb, John H.: III, 11

Bibbins, Ann: LB, 20
  John: LB, 20
Bibey, John: LB, 30
Birckhead, Edward F.: II, 175
  Elizabeth W.: II, 175
  Francis: II, 175, 197, 501
  Francis, Jr.: II, 197
  John: II, 203
  Mildred: II, 175
  Richard W.: II, 197, 203
  Susan F.: II, 175
  Thomas: II, 175, 203
Bishop, Barbara: LB, 79
  Elizabeth Caroline: II, 301
  Joseph: LB, 26, 46; II, 173, 195
  Reuben: LB, 79
  Robert: LB, 39
  William: II, 301
Black, Jacob: LB, 70
  Jonathan: LB, 2
  Sarah: LB, 70
Blackwell, James: III, 176
  Mildred: LB, 7
  William: III, 214
Bladden, Sarah: LB, 72
Blain, Alexander: II, 1
  Lucinda: II, 1
  Rush: LB, 18
Booth, George: LB, 27
  George W.: III, 254
  William: LB, 48
Boots, Thomas: LB, 10, 15
Bowcock, John J.: II, 233, 355, 543; III, 232
  J. J.: III, 96, 202
Bowen, Adeline: III, 56
  Ellen F.: III, 56
  Ephraim: II, 31
  Mary L.: III, 56
  Thomas C.: III, 7, 284
  Wilhelmina M.: III, 56
Bowles, Ann J.: II, 179
  Kitty: II, 179
Bowman, John: II, 397
Boyd, James: LB, 37
Bramham, Nimrod: LB, 56, 66, 76; II, 167, 307
Brand, Catharine: II, 201
  Catharine N.: II, 233
  Catharine Virginia: II, 307
  Chiles: II, 201, 233
  Chiles M.: II, 307; III, 222, 270
  Lucy E.: II, 233
  James W.: II, 233
  Maria: II, 201
  Maria L.: II, 233
  Maria Louisa: II, 307
  Richard A.: II, 233
  Robert: II, 233
  Sarah R.: II, 233

Brand, William W.: II, 233
Bransford, Owen C.: III, 264
Breckinridge, J.: LB, 3
Breedlove, Absolom W.: LB, 34
   Aylett: LB, 34
   Cornelius: LB, 7
   Jane: LB, 34, 56
   Madison: LB, 34, 56
   Polly: LB, 34
Brockenbrough, Arthur S.: LB, 69, 73
   Lucy: II, 353
Brockman, Aggy: LB, 29, 34, 50
   Ambrose: LB, 9, 11, 24, 28
   Blueford: LB, 29, 50
   Luford: LB, 34 [see Blueford]
   Julia A.: LB, 28, 29
   Samuel: LB, 24, 28, 29, 34, 50
   Sims: LB, 29, 34, 50
   Tandy: LB, 29, 34, 50
   Tazwell: LB, 29, 34, 50
   William: II, 11
Brooking, Robert U.: II, 373, 375
Brooks, James: LB, 3, 18, 19, 20, 23, 55, 60
   Richard W.: LB, 47, 52, 55, 69, 75, 76
Brown, Anderson: LB, 30; III, 54
   Andrew: LB, 24, 30, 53
   Angeline M.: II, 500, 541
   Benjamin T.: II, 537, 539
   Bernard: LB, 35; II, 231
   Bernis: LB, 25, 62
   Bezaleel: LB, 49; II, 193, 309, 433; III, 13
   Brightberry: LB, 68
   Burlington B.: II, 500
   Charles: LB, 35; II, 309; III, 13
   Charles G.: III, 24
   Clifton: II, 231
   Elijah: LB, 74
   Elizabeth: LB, 62
   Elizabeth D.: II, 231
   Garland T.: III, 5
   George B.: III, 134
   Ira B.: LB, 70, 72; II, 379, 500, 537, 539, 541, 543
   Jacintha C.: II, 500, 541
   James L.: II, 500, 543
   J. Augustus: III, 134
   Joel W.: II, 451
   John: LB, 47, 53; III, 24, 26, 142
   Margaret: LB, 53
   Marietta: III, 26, 142
   Martha E.: III, 26
   Mary: LB, 24
   Matthew: II, 285
   Matthew W.: II, 281
   Polly: LB, 30
   Samantha S.: II, 500, 539
   Sarah: LB, 35
   Sarah A.: II, 500, 537

Brown, Thomas H.: II, 215, 543
  Virginia F.: II, 500, 537
  William: LB, 49; II, 193
  William A.: III, 142, 160
  William H.: II, 467
  Williamson: LB, 24
Browning, Amanda: LB, 62
  Anny: LB, 62
  Elisha: LB, 62
  Elisha C.: II, 531; III, 28
  Jonathan: LB, 62
  Polly: LB, 62
  Susannah: LB, 62
  William: LB, 62
  William H.: III, 32
  Winney: LB, 62
Bruce, Ann E.: III, 96
  E. W.: III, 96
  George: LB, 6, 10, 16
  Nancy: III, 96
Bruffy, George: II, 227
  Strother: II, 227
Buckner, Phill: LB, 9, 12
Burger, George: LB, 9, 14
  John: LB, 60
Burgess, Glenford: II, 163
  John: II, 163
Burnley, Ann: LB, 46, 66
  Ann Elizabeth: II, 215
  Drury W.: III, 196, 232
  Francis: LB, 46
  James: LB, 46
  James F.: II, 503; III, 144, 258
  James H.: II, 215
  John: LB, 66
  Lewis B.: III, 19
  Nathaniel: LB, 66; II, 239, 241, 503; III, 3, 62, 216, 258
  Nicholas: LB, 67
  Sally H.: III, 62
  Seth: LB, 66; II, 215, 271, 273; III, 3, 292
  William R.: III, 62
Burrus, Charles: LB, 22, 26, 67; II, 95
  Dickenson: LB, 67
  Elizabeth: LB, 40, 67
  Isaac: LB, 40
  Justian: LB, 26
  Justiana: LB, 22
  Martha: LB, 40
Burton, Frances: II, 155
  Hudson: III, 64
  James: LB, 51, 55
  Mary F.: II, 155
  Richard N.: LB, 31
  Thomas: LB, 44; II, 339, 389, 395
  William C.: II, 155, 507
Buster, Claudius: LB, 27
  Franklin: LB, 27

Buster, John: LB, 27, 43
Butler, Allerson: II, 37
Camden, John: LB, 42
  Marbell: LB, 42
  Nancy: LB, 42
  Sarah: LB, 42
Camp, Ambrose: LB, 70
  William: LB, 70
Campbell, Elizabeth: LB, 35
  John: LB, 35
  John R.: II, 9
  Sarah A.: II, 9
  Sylus: LB, 35
Carden, William F.: LB, 71
Carnahan, Frances V.: III, 28
  John W.: III, 28
Carr, Anderson G.: LB, 29
  Barnett: LB, 68
  Bernard: LB, 64; II, 243; III, 238, 240
  Dabney: LB, 22, 37, 57, 72; II, 101, 529
  Daniel F.: LB, 75
  David: LB, 40
  Ellen M.: II, 323
  Frank: II, 17, 49, 335, 337
  Garland: LB, 10, 17
  Gay Ferguson: II, 304
  George: LB, 10, 15, 40; II, 187, 189
  George W.: III, 238
  Gideon: LB, 44
  Henly: LB, 40
  James L.: II, 367, 445
  James O.: LB, 63, 75
  Jane: LB, 41
  John: LB, 3, 7, 10, 17, 33, 40, 41; II, 187, 189
  John A.: II, 304, 323, 367
  John A., Lieut.: II, 445
  John B.: LB, 72
  John F.: LB, 33
  John Gay: II, 445
  John M.: III, 26, 238, 240
  Jonathan B.: LB, 51
  Julia: II, 243
  Mechans: LB, 64
  Meed: LB, 68
  Mekins: LB, 68
  Micajah: LB, 3, 40, 68
  Nancy: III, 238, 240
  Nancy W.: III, 240
  Overton: III, 238, 240
  Overton W.: II, 243
  Peter: LB, 22
  Polly: LB, 64
  Rachel: LB, 64
  Sally D.: LB, 33
  Sally W.: III, 52
  Samuel: LB, 22, 34, 51; II, 304, 323, 367, 445; III, 52
  Sarah: LB, 40
  Shelby: II, 243

Carr, Thomas: LB, 9, 10, 11, 17, 34
   Thomas D.: LB, 33
   Thomas, Jr.: LB, 19
Carrell, Betsey: LB, 24
   John: LB, 24
Carsney [or Casney]
   Christopher: LB, 69
Carter, Ann W.: LB, 9, 11
   Burnett: III, 144
   Charles: LB, 9, 14; II, 139
   Charles B.: III, 144
   Edward: LB, 9, 14
   Hill: LB, 9, 14
   James H.: III, 144
   John C.: II, 139
   Mary C.: LB, 10, 16
   Robert: II, 139
   Thomas: LB, 58
   Whittaco: LB, 9, 14
   William T.: III, 144
Carthra[?], Charles: LB, 62
Carver, James: II, 479
   Reuben: II, 479
Casney [see also Carsney]
   Elizabeth: LB, 69
Catlett, George W.: LB, 45
   Kemp: LB, 45, 46
   Laurence T.: LB, 70
   Thomas K.: LB, 46
Catling, Joshua: LB, 20
Catterton, Michael: LB, 32; II, 493; III, 214
   Michael, Sr.: II, 297
   William, Jr.: II, 421
Chapman, James: II, 145
   James E.: III, 17, 72; III, 214
Cheatham, Sarah: II, 291
   William: II, 291
   William G. W.: II, 291
Chewning, John: III, 78
   John W.: II, 545
Childres, Samuel: LB, 81; II, 75
Chiles, Bushrod B.: II, 191
   Henry: LB, 67
Chisholm, Isham: LB, 39
   Lavinia Ann: III, 104
   Menucan: III, 104
   William: III, 104
Clark, see also Clarke
   Jacob: LB, 20
   James: LB, 20
   Jefferson: II, 17
   John, Jr.: LB, 6
   Micajah: LB, 3, 20
   Nancy: LB, 3
   Robert: LB, 3
   William: LB, 3, 20
Clarke, see also Clark
   Catharine A.: II, 383

Clarke, Henry J.: III, 288
   James: LB, 76
   Mary Jane: III, 232
   Parsons: LB, 71, 75
   Thomas: III, 232
   Thomas N.: II, 383
   William: LB, 9, 13, 14
   Woodson P.: LB, 51
Clarkson, Arramintha: LB, 66
   Arramintha W.: LB, 55, 57
   David: LB, 9, 10, 12, 13, 16, 48
   Elizabeth: LB, 48, 49
   Elizabeth Ann: LB, 70
   James: LB, 66
   John: LB, 20
   John N.: LB, 55, 57, 66
   Julius: LB, 49, 70
   Julius W.: LB, 55, 57, 66
   Manoah: LB, 55
   Nancy: LB, 48
   Peter: LB, 9, 12, 13
   Reuben: LB, 55, 57, 66
   William L.: LB, 55, 57, 66
Clayton, John: LB, 10, 15
Cleaveland [or Cleveland]
   Albert H.: III, 252
   Anne: LB, 26
   Benajah: LB, 52
   Jeremiah: LB, 7, 26, 52, 65, 66
   John: LB, 7
   Oliver: LB, 52, 56
   Reubin: LB, 7
   Salley: LB, 26
   William: LB, 52
Cloar, Mary: III, 282
Cobbs, Frances Ann: II, 363
   Louisa: II, 401
   Mary Frances: LB, 56
   Samuel: LB, 56; II, 337, 363, 401
   Thomas: LB, 45, 46
   Virginia: II, 401
Cochran, John: II, 443
Cocke, John S.: III, 34
Coffman, Joseph: LB, 47, 55
Coleman, Hawes: LB, 37
   John H.: II, 61, 345, 377, 471, 549, 551, 561
   Roderick S.: III, 220
   William Emmet: III, 220
Coles, Edward: III, 260
   Elizabeth: LB, 30
   Emily: LB, 30
   Isaac A.: LB, 30, 58
   John: LB, 1, 30
   Reuben: II, 37
   Sally: LB, 30
   Tucker: LB, 30, 58

Colston, Nannie F.: III, 246
  Raleigh: III, 246
  Susan C.: III, 246
  Thomas M.: III, 246
Colvard, Elizabeth: LB, 10, 16
Colvin, Alexander: LB, 56
  Susan: LB, 56
Cooke, Thomas J.: III, 278
Cooper, George: II, 107
  Louisa: II, 107
Craddock, John: LB, 53
Crank, George: II, 89
  George H.: III, 180
  John: LB, 71, 80; II, 223
Craven, Andrew J.: III, 156, 280
  Edmund J.: III, 156, 280
  Emma J.: III, 170
  Euphemia H.: III, 132
  George W.: III, 26, 38, 132, 150, 152, 154, 156, 170, 186
  James L.: III, 132
  Jesse L.: III, 152
  John D.: II, 137, 195; III, 154, 156, 170, 280
  Maria L.: III, 156, 280
  Mary R.: III, 154
  Peter H.: III, 152
  Sandy H.: III, 132
  Sarah L.: III, 132
  Susan C.: III, 156, 280
  Virginia H.: III, 132
  William L.: III, 132, 140, 170, 186
Crawford, Edwin S.: III, 186
  Flourance: III, 176
  George William: III, 176
  Isaac: III, 176
  James W.: III, 176, 178
  John H.: III, 150
  M. F.: III, 186
  Malcom F.: III, 150, 152, 154, 156
  Mary S.: III, 150
  Samuel: III, 176
  Virginia A.: III, 150
Crenshaw, Dorithy: II, 15
  William: II, 15; III, 124
Crewdson, James S.: III, 64
Cromwell, Jesse: II, 27
  Sarah Ann: II, 27
Crosthwait, Ann Bowen: LB, 9, 11
  Perry: LB, 9, 11
  Shelton: LB, 9, 11
  Thomas: LB, 7
  William: LB, 7
Curry, Sally: LB, 43
Dabney, William S.: III, 52
Dalton, William: LB, 10, 15
Darneille, Isaac: LB, 46
  John: LB, 46; II, 561
  Phillip A.: II, 561
  Sarah W.: II, 561

Darrow, Henry A.: II, 556
   Jane A.: II, 556
   Ludowick: II, 556
Davis, Ann M.: III, 162
   Asa: LB, 23
   Benjamin: LB, 23, 54
   Cornelia D.: II, 273
   Edmond: LB, 30, 63, 67, 81; II, 537
   Elizabeth S.: II, 271
   Eugene: II, 89, 335; III, 162
   Hugh: II, 521
   Isaac, Jr.: LB, 59; II, 271, 273
   Jacob: LB, 60
   James M. M.: III, 162
   John: LB, 60; II, 85, 285
   John A. G.: II, 69, 304, 335; III, 162
   Lewis: LB, 5
   Lewis, Jr.: LB, 5
   Robert: LB, 30
   Sally: LB, 5
   Sally H.: II, 271
   William T.: II, 521
Dawson, Allen: II, 47, 49
   Jane: III, 252
   Margaret P.: III, 252
   Martin: LB, 20
   Martin A.: II, 49
   Nelson: III, 252
   Rufus K.: II, 47
   William W.: II, 47, 451, 453, 457
Day, Lucy: LB, 71
   Nancy: LB, 48
   Polly: LB, 48
   Willis: II, 269
Denton, John: LB, 2
Dettor, Henry K.: II, 465
   James W.: II, 465
   John: II, 301
   John W.: II, 465
   Joseph: II, 299, 427, 437
   Martha Ann: II, 465
   Matthias: II, 465
   Nicholas M.: II, 465
   Sarah C.: II, 465
Dickenson, Barrett: LB, 66
   Douglass: LB, 66
   Greffa [Griffin]: LB, 24
   Griffin: LB, 25
   James: LB, 24, 25
   John: LB, 64, 66, 76
   Lucy: LB, 24, 25
   Thomas: LB, 24
   Wiley: LB, 24, 28, 29, 33, 50, 51; III, 84
Dickerson, Anne: LB, 57
   John: LB, 57
Digges, George P.: II, 493
   Malinda: II, 493
   Mary W.: II, 493

Divers, George: LB, 7, 8, 9, 11, 21
Dollins, Elizabeth: LB, 1
  Hugh: LB, 1
  Jeremiah: II, 283
  John: LB, 60; II, 283
  Martha: II, 283
  Mary Ann: II, 283
  Nicholas: II, 283
  Sally: II, 283
  Tyre [Tyree]: II, 283; III, 130
  William: LB, 1
Donaho, William: II, 339
Dossey, James: LB, 63
  Mary Ann Mildred: LB, 63
  Richard: LB, 63; III, 274
Doughy, John B.: III, 96
Douglass, James P.: III, 268
  John: LB, 57, 68
  Magil O.: III, 268
Dowell, Ambrose: LB, 4, 19
  James: LB, 19, 36, 38, 66, 68
  John: LB, 19
  Madison: II, 355
  Major: LB, 19
  Nancy: LB, 19
  Thomas: LB, 19
Downs [Douris?], Mary: LB, 53
Draffen, Peggy: LB, 26
  Thomas: II, 77
Drumheller, Daniel: LB, 50
  Jacob: LB, 50; II, 85
  James: LB, 50
  James W.: III, 160, 216
  John: LB, 50
  Leonard: III, 22
  Nicholas: LB, 50
  Ross: LB, 50
  Sarah: LB, 50; II, 85
Dudley, James: LB, 31, 43, 58
Duke, James: LB, 55; II, 181
  John: II, 279
  Martha R.: II, 279
  Richard: II, 23, 41, 271, 273
  Richard T. W.: III, 220
  William J.: II, 233
Dundoe, John: III, 118, 120
Dundore, John: III, 234
Dunkum, John: II, 29, 177, 179, 225
  William: II, 225
Dunn, James M.: III, 184
  Thomas R.: II, 379; III, 72
Durrett, Achilles: LB, 24
  Adeline: II, 421
  Columbia: II, 421
  Davis: LB, 59; II, 119
  Elizabeth: LB, 59
  Frances: II, 421
  Francis: LB, 59

Durrett, Isaac: LB, 59
   James: LB, 42; II, 79, 217, 219; III, 228
   Jane: II, 421
   John: LB, 59
   John D.: LB, 59
   Marcus: II, 101, 289; III, 58, 228
   Marshall: LB, 42, 62
   Matilda: LB, 59
   Milly: LB, 42
   Richard: LB, 1, 59; II, 79
   Richard M.: II, 295; III, 58, 228
   Richard Montgomery: II, 119
   Robert: II, 119
   Robert D.: II, 181
   Sarah: LB, 42, 59
   Susan Ann Eliza: II, 217, 219
   Thomas: LB, 59; II, 119, 421
   William: LB, 42
   William H.: II, 421
Dyer, Celia A.: III, 1
   Charles C.: III, 1
   Edward: II, 513
   Eliza: II, 513
   Francis B.: LB, 73, 77; II, 179; III, 1
   Gasway B.: III, 1
   Robert: II, 513
   Sally G.: III, 1
   Samuel: LB, 19, 22, 39; II, 513
   Samuel, Jr.: II, 513
   Samuel M.: III, 1
   Susan: II, 513
   Thomas B.: II, 513
Eades, George: LB, 69
Eagan, John: II, 427, 441
   Sampson: II, 441
Early, Elizabeth: II, 151
   Frances: II, 145
   James: LB, 32; II, 51, 53, 119, 379
   James T.: II, 147, 151, 399
   Jeremiah: II, 149
   Joab: II, 145
   John: II, 145, 147, 149
   Joseph R.: II, 147
   Margaret: II, 149
   William: II, 51, 53, 149
   William T.: III, 92, 194, 204, 214
Eastham, James: II, 243
Edge, Philip: III, 74
Edwards, Ambrose: LB, 9, 15
   Brice: LB, 57, 76
   Hiram G.: III, 268
   John D.: III, 268
   Martha: LB, 9, 15
   Thomas: LB, 68
Ellis, Bentley B.: III, 5
Elsom, Nelson W.: II, 325
   William: LB, 63, 72

Emmett, Jane Louisa: III, 15
   John P.: III, 15
   Mary Bird: III, 15
   Thomas Addis: III, 15
Esken, John: II, 57
   Mary: II, 57
Essex, Benjamin: LB, 72
   Joseph: II, 301
Eubank, Benjamin H.: III, 160
   Eliza M.: LB, 76
   Emily A.: LB, 76
   George: LB, 39, 41, 76
   Isaetta J.: LB, 76
   James: LB, 44, 46
   John: LB, 39, 76; II, 313, 435
   John, Sr.: LB, 41; II, 479
   Martha W.: LB, 76
   Mary P.: LB, 76
   Nelson K.: LB, 39
   Sally Key: LB, 41
   Thomas: LB, 44, 46
   Thomas T.: LB, 76
   Wilson: LB, 76
   Winifred: LB, 76
Eversole, Abraham: LB, 67
   Leah: LB, 67
Everett, Charles: LB, 21
Fadley, Thomas: II, 27
Fagg, John: LB, 76
Falwell, Samuel: II, 57
Faris, John: LB, 73
Farish, Benjamin: II, 57
   Thomas L.: III, 278
   William P.: II, 405, 519, 545; III, 34, 166, 195, 278
Farrar, John S.: II, 221, 223
   Joseph: II, 75
   Lavenia M.: II, 223
   Marcellus: II, 223
   Martha G.: II, 223
   Richard: LB, 27
   Richard L.: II, 221
   Sarah: II, 75
   Shelton: LB, 27
   Sophia J.: II, 223
   Thomas: III, 44
Fearneyhough [or Ferneyhough]
   Edward: LB, 68; II, 147, 151, 175, 265, 267, 365
   Elizabeth (Early): II, 151
   John E.: II, 151
   Sarah Eliza: II, 151
Fenwick, John W.: II, 485
Ferguson, Hawkey: LB, 40
   Wiley: LB, 40
Ferneyhough, see Fearneyhough
Ficklen [or Ficklin]
   Benjamin: LB, 67, 73; II, 405
Field, Joseph: LB, 40
   Ralph H.: LB, 43

Fisher, Elizabeth: III, 134
   Robert: III, 134
Fitch, William D.: LB, 50; II, 55, 425, 443
Fitzpatrick, Edward: LB, 18
Flannagan, Ambrose: LB, 10, 15
Flynt, William: LB, 1
Foster, Allen: LB, 65
   Christian: LB, 20, 25
   Hugh: III, 32
   James: LB, 20, 25
   Joel: LB, 55
   John A.: II, 283, 531
   John D.: II, 15
   Joshua: LB, 80
   Robert: LB, 80
   Sarah Shelton: LB, 25
   Susanna: LB, 20, 25
   Thomas: II, 467
   William: LB, 25
   William M.: III, 32
   Williamson: LB, 20
Fowler, Christopher L.: III, 218
Fox, Joseph: II, 117
Frailey, William: LB, 22, 26
Franklin, Bernerd: LB, 26
Fray, John: II, 329, 331, 373, 375
Fretwell, Ann C.: III, 284
   Bernard: III, 3
   Brightberry: III, 3
   Crenshaw: LB, 54, 67
   Elizabeth: III, 3
   Franklin: III, 3
   Hudson: LB, 49; III, 3
   Jemima: LB, 67
   Jeramy: III, 3
   Vienna L.: III, 284
   William: LB, 49
   William, Jr.: LB, 67
   William C.: III, 284
Fry, Mary: LB, 53
   Reubin: LB, 53
Gamble, William: LB, 71
Gantt, Albert W.: III, 116
   Henry: III, 116
   John: II, 75
Gardner, Cynthia Ann: III, 5
   Jemima: LB, 32
   Nancy: LB, 32
   Wilson: III, 5
Garland, Anderson: LB, 58
   Burr: LB, 65
   Clifton: LB, 26
   Goodridge: II, 99
   Hudson: LB, 5
   James: LB, 65; II, 99, 161
   James, Jr.: LB, 5
   Maurice H.: LB, 65
   Nathaniel: LB, 58
   Nicholas A.: LB, 65

Garland, Peter: LB, 69, 70; II, 99, 161
  Rice: LB, 26, 65
  Robert: LB, 58, 74
  Samuel: LB, 65; II, 229
  William: LB, 65, 74
  William V.: II, 127
Garner, Alphonzo: II, 279
  Mary: LB, 67
  Sarah: LB, 67
  William G.: LB, 67
Garrett, Alexander: LB, 29, 37, 45, 46, 49, 50, 54, 62, 70, 77, 81;
  II, 349; III, 190
  George W.: III, 190
  Ira: LB, 8, 18; II, 25, 45, 211; III, 190
Garrison, Achilles: LB, 64
  Charles L.: II, 125
  Elijah: LB, 64
  Eliza: LB, 64
  Frank: III, 270
  Ira Chapman: III, 270
  James: LB, 64
  John: LB, 73, 75; II, 125
  Kelly: LB, 64
  Levina: LB, 73
  Lewis: III, 270
  Martha: III, 270
  Mary Ann: LB, 75
  Nancy: LB, 64
  Ralph: III, 270
  Samuel: LB, 34
  William: III, 270
Garth, B. B.: III, 248
  Brightberry B.: II, 129; III, 230
  Burwell G.: II, 271
  Elijah: LB, 25
  Garland: LB, 54; II, 119, 271, 273
  Garland A.: III, 62, 158, 164, 196
  James D.: III, 158, 164, 196
  Jesse: LB, 58; II, 129, 433
  Jesse T.: II, 433
  Jesse W.: LB, 50
  Martha C.: II, 129
  Mary E.: II, 129
  Susan C.: III, 158, 164, 196
  Thomas: LB, 31
  Virginia Eliza: II, 129
  Walter G.: III, 158, 164, 196
  William: III, 80, 88, 208
  Willis D.: II, 383
Gates, John: II, 205
Gay, John: LB, 71
  Samuel S.: II, 435
  Thomas: II, 435
  Thomas H.: II, 435
  William C.: III, 256
Gentry, Amanda: II, 531
  Claybourn: LB, 42
  David: LB, 35, 72; II, 29

Gentry, Enock: II, 531
  Henry: III, 184
  James C.: III, 262
  Jane: III, 184
  John: III, 184
  Josiah: LB, 9, 13
  Nicholas: LB, 45
  Parmelia E.: II, 29
  Pascal: III, 184
  Sarah: III, 184
George, James: LB, 10, 16
  John: III, 256
Gianniny, Nicholas: II, 163
Gibbons, John M.: II, 353
  Margaret N.: II, 353
Gibson, Andrew W.: III, 100
  Barbara A.: III, 274
  George J.: **LB**, 74; III, 274
  John: III, 100, 274
  John W. C.: III, 274
  Nancy E.: III, 274
  Sandy: III, 274
Gilbert, Thomas: II, 365
Gillaspy [or Gillaspie]
  David: LB, 7
  John: LB, 34
  Lewis: LB, 34
  Susan: LB, 34
Gillock, Benjamin: LB, 42
  Robert: LB, 42
Gillum, **Bennett**: LB, 40
  Frederick: LB, 52; II, 315
  James: LB, 80
  Jeremiah: LB, 40
  John: LB, 3, 32, 48
  Nancy: LB, 10, 16
  Pleasant: LB, 51
  Rebecca: LB, 32
  Sarah: LB, 10, 16
  Siotha: LB, 40
  Susannah: LB, 32
  William: LB, 3
Gilmer, Ann H.: II, 69
  George: LB, 19, 21, 22, 36; II, 133
  George, Doctor: LB, 22
  George C.: II, 69, 477, 491; III, 104, 136
  Harmer: LB, 21
  James: LB, 19
  John: LB, 74, 81; II, 69
  John H.: II, 69, 477
  Lucy: LB, 21
  Lucy W.: II, 69
  Maria J.: II, 69
  Martha J.: II, 69
  Sarah E.: III, 136
  Susannah F.: LB, 22
  Thomas W.: II, 69, 93, 207
  Zachariah: III, 136

Gilmore, Elizabeth: II, 61, 261
  Elizabeth E.: II, 481
  Frances: II, 61
  John: II, 61, 261
  John E.: II, 485
  Martha: II, 61, 261, 485
  Rebecca: II, 61, 261
  William: II, 61, 261, 481, 485
Gladden, Edward H.: LB, 50
Gooch, Edwin H.: III, 54
  Thomas W.: II, 65
Goodin, Polly: II, 305
  William: II, 305
Goodloe, Addison M.: III, 106
  James: III, 106
  John: III, 106
  John H.: III, 106
  Lucy: III, 106
  Mary: III, 106
  Sally: III, 106
  Spotswood: III, 106
  Thomas H.: III, 106
Goodman, David R.: III, 36, 292
  Horsley: LB, 10, 16, 29, 33, 59
  Jeremiah A.: LB, 57
  Letitia A.: III, 36
  Nathan C.: II, 299, 309, 459; III, 36
  Sarah W.: III, 36
  William: II, 217, 219, 459, 503
Goodridge, Catherine: LB, 51
  Fleet: LB, 55
  John: LB, 51, 55
  Lucy: LB, 55
Goolsby, Nathaniel: II, 221, 223
Goss, Ebenezer: II, 341
  John: II, 341
  John W.: II, 341
  William W.: II, 341
Grady, Jesse: LB, 27
  Joshua: LB, 27
Grass, Jacob: LB, 23, 77
  John: LB, 77
Graves, William: III, 252, 290
Gray, Harriet: LB, 69
  Rebecca: LB, 73
  William: LB, 69, 73
Grayson, John: III, 182
  Joseph: III, 182
  Mary Frances: III, 182
  Patsy: LB, 40
  Sarah: LB, 43
  Thomas: LB, 40, 43
  Thomas H.: III, 182
  William: LB, 4
  William D.: III, 182
Greening, Robert: LB, 4
  Sally: LB, 4

INDEX, page 19

Grimes, Polly: II, 59
Grymes, William: LB, 41
Grinstead, James: II, 441
    James H.: II, 427, 441; III, 7
    Jane: II, 441
    Joseph: II, 441
    Joseph A.: II, 427; III, 7
    J^s H.: III, 7
    Mary Jane: II, 427; III, 7
    Richard: II, 441
    Richard D.: III, 7
    Richard J.: II, 427
    Sarah: II, 427
Gunter, Austin: LB, 36
    John: LB, 36
Gypson, Randolph: II, 73
Hackley, Richard: LB, 26
Haden, Benjamin: LB, 74
    William: II, 105
Halbach, John P.: II, 157
Hall, John: LB, 72; II, 281, 285; III, 128
    John R.: III, 128
    Lucy R. R.: III, 128
    Nicholas: LB, 52
    Richard: II, 281
    Robert: II, 159
    William: LB, 9, 15
    William D.: II, 285
Ham, Dolly: II, 265
    Doratha: II, 365
    Edward: II, 365
    Elijah: II, 265, 267, 365
    Granville: II, 265
    Granville A.: II, 267
    James: II, 267
    Joab: II, 267
    Samuel: II, 265, 365
    Susan: II, 265, 365
    Thomas: II, 265, 365
Hamner, Charles W.: LB, 23; II, 29
    Elizabeth: LB, 23, 80
    Henly: LB, 23
    Jesse B.: II, 325
    John: LB, 35, 72
    Rachel J.: LB, 22
    Samuel: LB, 23
    Sarah: LB, 35
    Susan: LB, 72
    Warwick W.: II, 339
    William: LB, 80
Hardin, Benjamin: LB, 54
Harlow, Nathaniel: LB, 9, 10, 12, 17
Harper, Gabriel: II, 287
    Gabriel S.: III, 42, 102
    William: LB, 79
Harris, Anderson: LB, 38
    Benjamin: LB, 27
    Edmond: LB, 42

Harris, Francis: LB, 37
  George W.: II, 289; III, 50
  Henry: III, 212
  Henry T.: LB, 60
  Ira: II, 77, 123
  James: LB, 1
  John: LB, 19, 23, 43, 46, 62, 68
  Larkin: LB, 45
  Mary A.: LB, 37
  Mathew C.: LB, 37
  Samuel W.: LB, 63
  Skiler: LB, 37
  Sophia: LB, 37
  Thomas: LB, 44
  Thomas W.: II, 123
  William: LB, 42, 44, 45
  William A.: LB, 63
Hart, Andrew: LB, 9, 13, 37, 68
  Ann Eliza: II, 371
  Elizabeth: LB, 9, 13
  Frances J.: II, 371
  James: II, 5, 7, 247
  John B.: III, 1
  Mary: LB, 9, 13
  Mary S.: II, 371
  Samuel J.: II, 371
  Samuel L.: LB, 9, 13, 48, 57, 59, 68
  Schuyler A.: II, 371
  William D.: II, 1, 5, 7, 479; III, 58
Harvard, John: II, 43
Hauss [Haws], Silas: III, 78
Hawley, James O.: II, 535; III, 19, 212
Haws, Daniel: II, 405
  Daniel M.: II, 545; III, 78
  John W.: II, 545
  John William: II, 405
Hays, Dulcema: II, 205
  Isaac: LB, 47
  James: LB, 47, 69, 76
  James, Jr.: LB, 44
  James, Sr.: LB, 44
  James J.: II, 429
  John: LB, 44, 58, 69; II, 205
  John D.: II, 429
  Louisa Jane: II, 429
  Malinda: LB, 76
  Nathaniel: LB, 44
  Nicholas D.: II, 429
  Sarah Ann: LB, 69; II, 429
  Thomas: LB, 47
  William: II, 429
Head, Edgar: III, 286
  Henry E.: III, 288
  Martha J.: III, 286
  Oscar W.: III, 286
  Valentine: III, 288
  William S.: III, 286
Heiskell, Jesse L.: III, 50

Henderson, Charles: LB, 9, 11
   Elizabeth: LB, 9, 11
   Francis: LB, 9, 11
   Hillsmon: LB, 9, 11
   Isham: LB, 9, 11
   James: LB, 9, 11
   James P.: LB, III, 147
   John: LB, 6, 9, 11
   Lucy: LB, 9, 11
   Margaret C.: III, 147, 148, 224
   Matthew: LB, 20
   Nancy: LB, 9, 11
   Sally: LB, 9, 11
   Susannah: LB, 6
   William: LB, 9, 11
Hening, William W.: LB, 18
Herndon, Amanda M.: II, 325
   Benjamin: III, 268
   Elisha M.: III, 282
   John M.: II, 325
   Reuben: II, 325
   Thompson: II, 389
Herrard, Nancy: LB, 50
   Voluntine: LB, 50
Hicks, David: II, 343
   Isaac: II, 269
Higgenbotham, William T.: II, 505
Hill, Ambrose B.: II, 193
   Durrett M.: II, 193
   John: LB, 77; II, 193
   Nancy E.: II, 193
   Sarah: II, 193
Hilton, Thursday Jenetta: II, 451
   William: II, 451
Hogg, William: LB, 42, 79
Holeman [or Holman]
   John T.: LB, 81; II, 61, 75
   Leonadas: LB, 77
Holmes, William: LB, 18
Hopkins, James: II, 105
   Margaret: II, 105
   Sally: LB, 10, 17
   Stephens D.: III, 58
   William: LB, 80
Hord, George M.: III, 180
   Lewis: III, 180
Hudson, Agness E.: II, 533
   Charles: LB, 23; II, 533; III, 146
   Christopher: LB, 39, 41, 54
   Isaetta: II, 533
   Iscietta L.: III, 146
   John: LB, 22, 23
   Larkin: LB, 38, 80; II, 289
   Sarah: LB, 22
   Sarah A.: II, 533
Hughes, Elijah: II, 403
   Elizabeth: II, 403
   Frances E.: II, 403

INDEX, page 22

Hughes, Lilbourn: II, 403
   Merial: II, 403
   William: II, 403
   William L.: II, 403
Humphrey, Andrew J.: II, 65
   Isaiah: II, 65
   Richard: LB, 67
   Spicer: LB, 67
Hunt, Benjamin: LB, 46
   Mary: LB, 46
Hunton, Thomas: LB, 42
Hurt, James: LB, 58; II, 63, 71, 227
   William: LB, 58
Hutchens, David: LB, 80
   Frances C.: LB, 80
Irvin, Samuel: LB, 60
Jackson, Thomas: II, 293
Jameson, William: LB, 42, 44, 45
Jarman, Dabney M.: II, 231
   Elizabeth M.: LB, 60
   James: LB, 33, 35, 57, 60, 70
   William: LB, 60
   William P.: III, 248
Jarrett, Isham: LB, 28
   Lidy: LB, 28
Jefferson, Robert L.: III, 116
Jeffries, Alfred K.: III, 210
   David W.: III, 210
   Harriet C.: II, 497
   James: II, 497; III, 210
   John: II, 319
   William: II, 497; III, 210
Johnson, Addison: II, 155
   Benjamin: LB, 43, 64
   Collin: II, 359
   Eliza: LB, 64
   Fleming: LB, 64
   Joshua: II, 155
   Joshua W.: II, 287
   Michael: LB, 74; II, 461
   Richard: LB, 10, 17
   Richardson: LB, 27
   Samuel S.: II, 269
   Stephen: II, 269
   Thomas: LB, 53
   William: LB, 34
   William L.: II, 287
Johnston, Horace Buckner: II, 503
   James M.: III, 54
   Joseph T.: II, 509
   Martha George: II, 503
   Mary Elizabeth: II, 503
   Richard H.: II, 503, 509
   William H.: II, 137, 345
Jones, Ann: III, 222
   D. N.: II, 223
   James: II, 385; III, 11
   James, Sr.: LB, 4

Jones, James J.: III, 26
   James W.: II, 535; III, 19, 212
   John: LB, 21, 56, 65, 73; III, 98
   John R.: LB, 76
   Mary: II, 385
   Thomas: II, 385, 535; III, 11, 19
   Thomas B.: III, 212
   Turner: III, 222
   William R.: LB, 21
Jopling, Cynthia: LB, 72
   Harriet: LB, 72
   James: LB, 24
   Jesse: II, 221, 223
Jouett, John: LB, 2
   Robert: LB, 6, 7
Keaton, Agness: II, 95
   Nelson: II, 95
Kelly, John: LB, 34, 54
Key, Jesse P.: LB, 39, 40, 41, 42
   John: LB, 4, 6, 10, 16
   Joshua: LB, 4, 10, 16, 20, 21, 32
   Martin: LB, 6
   Price: LB, 59
   Tandy: LB, 41
   Walter: LB, 6, 32
Kidd, John: III, 248
Kimbrough, Meredith: LB, 65
King, James: II, 351
Kinsolving, Amanda W.: II, 33
   Calvin: II, 255
   Celestria: II, 255
   George W.: LB, 63; II, 19, 33, 35, 65, 261, 309; III, 284, 288
   James: LB, 9, 15; II, 33, 35
   Jefferson B.: II, 33, 35
   Madison B.: II, 255
   Madison B. G.: II, 35
   Napoleon B. L.: II, 35
   Percilla: II, 255
Lacy, Charles C.: LB, 27, 79
Lama, Mary Ann: III, 262
   William: III, 262
Lane, Elizabeth: II, 393
   Sarah: III, 254
   Thomas: II, 3
   William: II, 393; III 254
Langford, Anderson: II, 495
   Parks: LB, 31
   [Landford], Parks B.: LB, 43
   West: II, 495
Laughlin, Sarah: II, 519
   Thomas C.: II, 519
Leake, Austin: LB, 53
   James: LB, 34
   Joseph S.: LB, 53
   Mary: LB, 9, 13
   Mask[?]: LB, 37
   Samuel: LB, 53
   Samuel A.: II, 511

Leake, Walter: LB, 5, 9, 13, 18
   William: LB, 49, 51, 53
Lee, George W.: LB, 9, 15
   John: III, 126
   Patsey M.: LB, 9, 15
   William: III, 126
Leigh, William: LB, 10, 17
Leitch, James: LB, 78, 79
   James A.: II, 453, 563; III, 126
   Martha Hay: II, 453
   Samuel: II, 107, 453
Lewis, Alice: LB, 76
   Alice L.: III, 138
   Charles: LB, 2, 3, 5, 10, 17
   Charles Warner: LB, 5
   Daniel: II, 533
   Daniel P.: III. 146
   David J.: LB, 50, 55
   Elizabeth: LB, 61
   Elizabeth D.: III, 138
   Ellen O.: III, 138
   Emeline: LB, 79
   George N.: III, 138
   Howell: LB, 2, 5, 79, 81
   Isham: LB, 2
   James: LB, 10, 16
   James Howell: II, 183
   Jane: LB, 2, 5, 54, 78
   Jesse: LB, 49, 70
   John, Jr.: LB, 22
   John W.: LB, 22, 79
   John Waddy: LB, 31
   Lydia: LB, 36
   Maria: LB, 79
   Mary Ann: LB, 54
   Mary Jane: LB, 79
   Mary Randolph: LB, 2
   Meriwether: LB, 2
   Nancy: LB, 9, 11, 54
   Nicholas: LB, 2, 76
   Nicholas H.: LB, 61, 78
   Peggy: LB, 29
   Polly: LB, 36
   Robert: LB, 78
   Robert W.: III, 138
   Samuel H.: II, 133
   Sarah E.: LB, 10, 17
   Susan: LB, 2
   Susanna: LB, 3
   Thomas F.: LB, 81; III, 42, 102
   Thomas W.: LB, 29, 36, 61, 76, 78
   William: LB, 2, 5
   Zac, Sr.: II, 533
   Zachariah, Jr.: II, 554
   Zachariah R.: II, 491; III, 146
Lindsay, Ann: II, 277, 457
   Henry: LB, 36
   James: II, 253, 275, 459; III, 38

Lindsay, Mary M.: II, 275, 277
   Reuben: II, 275, 277, 457, 459; III, 38
   William: II, 275, 459
Linton, Sarah: LB, 10, 15
Lively, Charles: LB, 63
   Patsey: LB, 43
Lobban, James: II, 67; III, 76, 280
   Jesse: II, 435
   John: II, 67
   John M.: II, 67
   Martha M. N.: III, 76
   Mary Ann: II, 67
   Washington P.: II, 67
   William F. N.: III, 76
Lott, Peter: LB, 19
Loving, Martha: LB, 62
   Randolph: LB, 62
Luck, Overton: LB, 76
   Patsey: LB, 76
Lupton, Jacob C.: LB, 56; II, 411, 413
Lyon, Ann: II, 425
   James W.: III, 160
   Samuel: II, 425
McAllester, James: II, 3
   James A.: II, 3
McBridee, John: LB, 53
McClung, William W.: III, 228
McCord, Alexander: II, 369
   Darkey: LB, 71
   Elizabeth J.: II, 369
   Sarah: LB, 80
   Sarah Elizabeth: II, 369
   William: LB, 71, 80
McCullock, Thomas: LB, 43
McDaniel, Elizabeth: III, 100
   Mary: LB, 69
   Sally: LB, 69
McGehee, Albert: II, 169
   Charles: II, 170
   Francis: LB, 56, 64; II, 463
   James: II, 169
   Joseph: II, 169, 170
   Mary: II, 170
   Mary L.: II, 169, 170
   Peter: III, 76, 112
   William: II, 169, 170
McKapon, William: II, 9
McLeod, Ann J.: II, 319
   Belinda: II, 319
   John W.: II, 319
   Richard T.: II, 319
   William: II, 319
Magruder, Allen B.: II, 558
   Allan R.: III, 220
   Benjamin H.: II, 137, 523
   Horatio J.: III, 78
   John T.: II, 558

Mahanes, Emmerly: LB, 34
  John: LB, 32
  Lewis: LB, 32, 34
  Meredith: LB, 32, 34
  Samuel: LB, 32
Mallory, Etta: II, 191
  Garland: LB, 62
  Thomas: II, 191
Marks, Elizabeth: LB, 8
  John: LB, 1, 28
  John H.: LB, 28, 36
  Martha: LB, 8
  Mary: LB, 28
  Mary C.: LB, 8
  Nancy: LB, 7
  Peter: LB, 7, 8
  Sophia: LB, 8
Marr [or Marrs, or Mars]
  Henry: LB, 77, 78
  James: LB, 73
  John: LB, 56, 65, 73, 79
  Nancy: LB, 56
  Peggy E.: LB, 65
  Pemily: LB, 78
  Rixin: LB, 77
  Sarah R.: LB, 79
  Thomas: LB, 77, 78
Marshall, Amanda M.: III, 174
  Bluford: III, 128
  Daniel W.: III, 174
  Epphroditus: III, 174
  George B.: III, 174
  Henry: II, 411, 413
  Henry P.: III, 174
  Isaac: II, 195, 201
  James: II, 11; III, 174
  John W.: III, 174
  Mary E.: III, 174
  Mildred A.: II, 11
  Patsey: LB, 64
  Polly: LB, 64
  Susan F.: III, 174
  Thomas: LB, 64
Martin, Benjamin: LB, 43, 61, 70, 77, 78; II, 39, 81; III, 276
  Caroline: LB, 77
  Cary: LB, 55
  Celia: LB, 61
  Elisha: LB, 61, 65
  Elizabeth C.: II, 143
  Elizabeth L. W.: LB, 50
  Emily: II, 81
  George: LB, 44, 50
  Hudson, Jr.: LB, 25
  James: LB, 55
  John: LB, 78; II, 39, 143, 161, 385; III, 276
  John L.: II, 143
  John M.: LB, 36, 41, 77, 79, 80
  Lindsay: LB, 70; II, 143

Martin, Lucy: II, 127
  Malinda W.: LB, 44
  Mary: II, 37
  Mary Ann: LB, 55
  Nicholas M.: LB, 79
  Peter: LB, 27
  Reuben H.: LB, 65
  Samuel: II, 37
  Samuel W.: II, 556
  Sarah: III, 276
  Thomas: LB, 44, 55; II, 127
  William H.: LB, 61
Mason, Edward S.: II, 551
  James M.: III, 30
  Sarah: II, 549
  Valentine M.: II, 549, 551; III, 30
Massie, Hardin: II, 45, 55
  Nathaniel H.: III, 280
Mathews, Charles: LB, 61
  Emma A.: III, 118
  Harriet: III, 118, 120
  Harriet A.: III, 118
  John: III, 120
  Joseph: III, 118
  Martha A.: III, 118
  Mary E.: III, 118
  Richard: III, 118, 120
  William: LB, 61; III, 120
Maupin, Addison: III, 272
  Ambrose: II, 369
  Betsy: LB, 73
  Chapman: LB, 75
  Chapman W.: LB, 68; II, 307, 309; III, 272
  Charles Smith: III, 272
  Daniel: LB, 9, 13, 42, 44, 45
  Daniel L.: II, 363
  David: LB, 73; II, 363
  Fontaine: LB, 75
  Gabriel: LB, 77, 78; III, 184
  John: LB, 33, 73
  M. R.: II, 539
  Martha: III, 192
  Mary Ann Sarah: LB, 78
  Nicholas: II, 95
  Polly: LB, 73
  Polly M.: LB, 33
  Rice: II, 243
  Thomas: LB, 73, 75; II, 33; III, 192
  William A.: III, 272
Maury, Francis F.: LB, 53
  Mathew: LB, 53
  Reuben: LB, 70
Maxwell, Bezaleel: LB, 68, 71, 75
  Isabella: LB, 54
  Jane: LB, 54, 68, 75
  John: LB, 54
  Robert B.: LB, 41
  Thomas: LB, 35, 41

Maxwell, William: LB, 68, 71
Mayo, John W.: II, 159
Meeks, Barttelott: LB, 2
   Martin: LB, 2
   Nancy: LB, 2
   Nelson: LB, 2
Melton, David: LB, 1
   Eli: LB, 1
   John: LB, 1
   John, Jr.: LB, 1
   Mary: LB, 1
   William: LB, 1
Merewether, Charles J.: II, 111, 555
Meriwether, Francis: II, 555
   Mary M.: II, 555
   Thomas W.: II, 251, 555
   W. H.: II, 49
   William: LB, 2
   William D.: LB, 10, 17, 19, 22, 29, 36; II, 251
Merritt, James: II, 257
   Markwood: II, 257
   Nicholas: II, 257
Michie, Adiline: III, 206
   Alexander H.: III, 204
   Augustus: III, 206
   Catharine F.: III, 90
   Chapman J.: II, 333
   Cornelia E.: III, 90
   David: II, 493
   Eugene O.: III, 92, 214
   Frances: II, 89; III, 80
   Frances A.: III, 88, 94
   Francis D.: II, 333
   Franklin J.: II, 333
   Henry Clay: III, 208
   James: LB, 33; II, 89, 333; III, 80, 88, 92, 204, 206, 208
   James, Jr.: III, 90, 92, 94, 214
   John A.: LB, 29, 31, 33
   John E.: II, 333; III, 204, 206
   John J.: III, 80, 88
   John P.: II, 333
   Jonathan: II, 333
   Joseph P.: III, 92
   Lucian A.: III, 92, 214
   Mary J. M.: II, 333
   Octavius G.: III, 90, 94
   Orin: III, 214
   Orvin: III, 92
   Patrick: LB, 33
   Susan F.: III, 208
   Theodore A.: III, 90
   Theresha: III, 206
   Thomas G.: III, 204
   Thomas W.: II, 333
   Virginia Ann: III, 94
   William: II, 89, 333; III, 206
   William J.: II, 137

Miller, Isaac: LB, 19, 22
  Jesse: LB, 60
  Polly: LB, 60
Mills, David: II, 539
  David W.: III, 198
  Elizabeth F.: LB, 30
  Frances: LB, 37
  James: LB, 58
  John: LB, 29, 37
  Joseph: LB, 7, 29
  Menan: LB, 2, 5, 6, 9, 15, 37
  Patsey: LB, 58
  Peggy: LB, 37
  Salley: LB, 30
  William: LB, 37
  Wilson: LB, 29
  Wyatt: LB, 29, 30
Minor, Betty [Elizabeth] Lewis: II, 527
  Catharine: LB, 81
  Dabney: LB, 10, 15, 29, 34, 46, 50, 63, 69, 81; II, 499
  Franklin: II, 235, 237
  George C.: II, 209
  Hugh: II, 209, 235, 237
  James: LB, 10, 15; II, 499
  John: LB, 10, 15; II, 349
  John, Jr.: II, 499
  John S.: II, 237
  Mary Louisa: II, 235
  Lucian: II, 157, 415
  Lucy Ellen: II, 415
  Maria: II, 415
  Mary M.: II, 415
  Mildred: LB, 81
  Nancy: LB, 10, 15
  Peter: LB, 34, 81; II, 209, 235, 237
  Peter C.: II, 209
  Samuel O.: LB, 61; II, 527
  Sarah: LB, 10, 17, 81
  Virginia L.: II, 415
  Warner W.: II, 415
  William W.: LB, 81; II, 349; III, 52, 82
Montgomery, Thomas: LB, 21
Moon, Ann M.: II, 137
  Anne M. W.: II, 345
  Ann Maria: II, 471
  Charlotte: III, 40
  Charlotte D.: II, 137, 345, 471
  Edward H.: II, 293, 471
  Elizabeth A.: II, 137
  Elizabeth M.: II, 345
  Fleming: II, 377
  Fleming B.: LB, 65
  Frances: II, 377
  Isaac D.: II, 345
  J. W.: II, 471
  Jacob: LB, 38, 65; II, 137, 345, 377, 471; III, 40

Moon, John D.: II, 109, 137, 345
  John D., Jr.: III, 58
  Littleberry: LB, 38; II, 91, 293
  Lorna: III, 40
  Martha L.: II, 137, 345, 471
  Martha P.: II, 91
  Mary M.: II, 137, 345, 471
  Mary P.: II, 293
  Mildred P.: II, 293
  Nathaniel: II, 377
  Richard: LB, 65, 66
  Richard, Sr.: LB, 38
  Samuel H.: LB, 38
  Samuel O.: II, 91, 293; III, 60
  Samuel W.: LB, 66
  Skiler: LB, 38
  Thomas: LB, 80
  William: LB, 38, 68
Moore, Anne: LB, 27
  Benjamin: II, 31, 59, 131, 227, 447, 449, 475
  Edward: LB, 2, 3, 6, 9, 10, 11, 17, 27
  Elizabeth: LB, 48, 74
  Henry C.: II, 101, 289, 383; III, 24, 58, 142
  Jane: LB, 23
  John: II, 339
  John L.: LB, 27
  L. R.: LB, 23
  Martin: LB, 30
  Morris: LB, 47
  Nancy: LB, 42
  Nancy T.: II, 447
  Richard: LB, 47, 66
  William: LB, 42, 48, 74
Moorman [or Mooreman]
  Dorothy: LB, 43, 81
  Elizabeth A.: LB, 81
  Elizabeth Ann: LB, 43
  Mary L.: LB, 43, 81
  Robert: LB, 43, 81
  Robert J.: LB, 81
  Robert James: LB, 43
Morris, Ann C.: III, 162
  Ann D.: II, 309
  Hugh Rice: LB, 56
  Jacob: LB, 56
  James A.: III, 136
  Jane: LB, 56
  John: LB, 56; II, 75, 213; III, 30
  Joseph W.: II, 323
  Nancy D.: II, 101
  Sopha: LB, 56
  William: II, 101, 289, 309; III, 58
  William M.: II, 289, 309; III, 58
  William Marshall: II, 101
Morrison, John Norborne: II, 554
Morrow, John: III, 212

Mosby, Benjamin: II, 487; III, 166
    Hezekiah: III, 166
    John: II, 487; III, 166
    Martha B.: III, 166
Moyer, John: LB, 48
Mullins, Ann B.: LB, 70
    Anthony: LB, 63
    Frances Jarman: LB, 57
    John: LB, 1, 5, 70
    John, Jr.: LB, 57
    Nancy: LB, 63
Munday [or Mundy]
    Abram: LB, 52
    Archibald: II, 355
    Archy: II, 407
    Delitha: II, 355
    Eliza: LB, 52
    Elizabeth: II, 117
    Henry: II, 355
    Mary: II, 407
    Meredith: II, 355, 407
    Nancy: LB, 52
    Samuel: LB, 4
    Telitha Ann: II, 407
Myers, Christopher: LB, 38
    Dicy: LB, 38
Nailor [or Naylor]
    Mildred: LB, 57
    Polly: LB, 57
    Sarah Rosanna: LB, 57
    Susannah: LB, 57
    Thomas: LB, 57, 61
Nelson, Ann Fitzhugh: LB, 29
    Caroline: II, 251
    Francis K.: II, 253
    Frank K.: II, 555
    Hugh: LB, 29; II, 251, 253
    Keating S.: II, 253; III, 200
    Robert: LB, 29
    Robert W.: II, 253
Newcomb, Ellen: II, 299
    John: II, 299
    Sarah: II, 299
Nicholas, John: LB, 6, 9, 10, 11, 16
    John H.: II, 549, 551
    Wilson C.: LB, 9, 10, 11, 16; III, 30
Noel, Catharine: II, 109
    Eli: LB, 62
    Elizabeth: II, 109
    Mary Jane: II, 87
    Thompson: II, 87, 109
Norris, Elizabeth Ann: III, 68
    Claudius E.: III, 68
    Columbia A.: III, 68
    Eliza R.: II, 489
    Eugene: III, 68
    Evalina: III, 172
    Jacob: LB, 76

Norris, James: II, 489; III, 230
   James H.: III, 70
   John: II, 153
   Joseph: II, 153
   Opie: LB, 76; II, 153, 489; III, 172
   Sallie T.: III, 172
   Samuel: III, 68
   Thomas A.: III, 72
   Thomas C.: III, 68, 70, 72, 230
Norvell, Benjamin: LB, 35, 41
   Caty: LB, 35
   James: LB, 71, 75
   John: LB, 35
   Sally C.: LB, 41
Oaks, Hudson: III, 130
Oglesby, Jacob: LB, 3, 6
   Pleasant: LB, 6
Old, Ann Patience: LB, 49
   George W.: LB, 49, 74
   James: LB, 28, 35, 45, 49, 50, 53
   John: LB, 44, 49, 74
   Nancy W.: LB, 44
   Thomas J.: LB, 49, 74
Oliver, George W.: LB, 77
Pace, Benjamin: II, 351
   Elizabeth F.: II, 195, 487
   Evalina B.: II, 195
   Evalina Bolling: II, 487
   George: LB, 63
   Harry: II, 195
   Henry T.: II, 487
   Joseph: II, 487
   Louisa Jane: II, 195, 487
   Lucy T.: II, 195, 487
Page, Edmond: LB, 25
Parish, Nancy: III, 64
   Samuel: III, 64
Pates, ____: II, 157
   Ellen W.: II, 157
Patrick, Charles: LB, 43
   John: LB, 43
   Washington: LB, 43
Payne, George B.: II, 513
   James M.: II, 1
   Nathaniel W.: II, 505
   Robert N.: II, 505
Peake, Mary J.: II, 225
   William: II, 225
Pemberton, Henry: LB, 55
Pence, Alexander: II, 443
   Beatriss: II, 443
Perkins, Benjamin M.: II, 93, 395; III, 116
   Daniel H.: III, 168
   Jane Lewis: III, 168
   Joseph: III, 168
Perry, John M.: LB, 46, 69, 76; II, 27
Pettit, Thomas: LB, 20
Pettitt, Sydner R.: II, 43

Peyton, Craven: LB, 22; II, 275, 277
Phelps, Charles: III, 160, 216
    Sarah M.: III, 160, 216
Phillips, Frances: LB, 20
    Philip: LB, 27, 63, 71
    Robert: LB, 18
    Stephen: LB, 20
    Susanna: LB, 20
    William B.: III, 264, 266
Pilson, John: LB, 80
Piper, Elizabeth: II, 165
    Garrett W.: II, 223
    Marshall: II, 295
    Mary Ann: II, 165
    William: II, 165, 295
    Willis W.: II, 295
Pleasants, Elizabeth Ann: III, 44
    Harriet: III, 44
    Jane: LB, 72
    John: LB, 60
Poates, Caroline M.: II, 557
    Elizabeth M.: II, 557
    Emily A. J.: II, 557
    John L.: II, 557
    Lewis L.: II, 557
Poindexter, James W.: II, 311
Points, James Williams: III, 282
Pollard, Edward A.: III, 147, 148, 224
    Henry R.: III, 147, 148
    James R.: III, 147, 148, 224
    Lucy E.: III, 147, 148
    Richard: III, 147, 148
    Virginia: III, 147, 148
Porter, Peter: II, 105, 261
Powell, Casper: II, 483
    Eliza A.: III, 248, 290
    Henry: LB, 25
    Michael: II, 343
    Samuel: LB, 28; II, 483; III, 248, 290
    Samuel M.: II, 483
    Thomas A.: III, 248, 290
    Walter M.: III, 248, 290
    William: II, 397
Price, Billy P.: III, 42
    Charles H.: III, 42
    Daniel: III, 42
    John: LB, 52
    Robert A.: III, 42, 102
    Sally A.: III, 42
    Stephen C.: III, 42, 102
Priddy, Eliza E.: III, 122
    John: III, 122
Proctor, Hannah: LB, 61
    Joseph B.: II, 43
    Mary: II, 43
Quarles, Albert: II, 349
    Henry: II, 349
    Lucy: II, 349

Quarles, Matilda: II, 349
Ragland, John C.: II, 361
   John K.: II, 361
   John R.: II, 361
   William N.: II, 361; III, 218
Railey, Carter H.: III, 54
   Catharine: LB, 38
   Charles: LB, 36
   Daniel: LB, 39
   Daniel M.: II, 47
   Elizabeth: LB, 36, 39
   John M.: LB, 36; III, 54
   Kitty C.: LB, 36
   Lilburn R.: LB, 36
   Martha J.: III, 54
   Martin: LB, 36, 38, 39
   Mary E.: III, 54
   Randolph: LB, 36
   William M.: III, 54
Ramsey, William: LB, 43, 58
Randal, John: LB, 38
Randolph, Benjamin F.: III, 86
   G. W.: III, 278
   George W.: III, 86
   Lewis: II, 259
   Thomas J.: II, 259, 431; III, 86, 190
   Thomas M.: LB, 31
Rea, Blan: III, 290
Reinhart, Catharine H.: III, 82
   E. W.: III, 82
   Ha___: III, 82
Rice, Claiborne: II, 409
   Holeman: LB, 37, 51; II, 511
   Jane: LB, 37
   Lucy: LB, 51
   William H.: II, 511
Richards, Fontaine: III, 198
   Franklin B.: III, 198
   George W.: III, 198
   John S.: III, 198
   Joseph R.: III, 198
   Martha A.: III, 198
Richardson, Henry W.: LB, 74
   Samuel: LB, 74
Ricks, Gilbert: II, 477
   Josias: II, 477
Rife, John: LB, 21, 24, 47
Riley, Joshua: LB, 48
Rippeto, Mary: II, 31
   Peter: II, 31
Rittenhouse, Henry: II, 439
   James: II, 439
Ritter, Samuel: LB, 56
Rives, Alexander: II, 423; III, 172, 174
   George: II, 423; III, 172
   George C.: II, 423
   James Henry: II, 423
   Robert: III, 147
   Robert C.: II, 423

Rives, William C.: LB, 80; II, 253
Roberts, Alexander: LB, 25
   James: LB, 52
   Malinda: LB, 52
   Richard: LB, 52
   William R.: II, 539
   Wilson: LB, 56, 65, 79
Robertson, Ann: LB, 49
   Cosby M.: II, 473
   William: LB, 49
   William J.: II, 221; III, 278
Robinson, Benjamin: LB, 30; II, 11
   James: LB, 9, 12, 27
   William: LB, 9, 12
Rodes, Ann D.: II, 309
   Clifton: LB, 37
   John: LB, 35, 57; II, 309
   Mathew: LB, 7, 20, 64
   Milly: LB, 10, 16
   William: II, 309
Rogers, Achilles: LB, 81
   Alexander H.: II, 247
   Benjamin F.: II, 473
   Celia B.: II, 245
   Elizabeth A.: II, 247
   Giles B.: III, 108
   James B.: II, 21; III, 9, 17, 90, 108, 194
   John: LB, 20, 81; II, 247
   John A.: II, 245
   Jonathan B.: II, 473
   Joseph: LB, 81
   Julia A.: II, 245
   Keziah S.: II, 473
   Margaret: II, 245, 247
   Parmenas: LB, 26; III, 108
   Susan E.: II, 247
   Thomas L.: III, 108
   Thompson: II, 473
   Thornton: II, 245, 247
   Thornton O.: II, 245
   William A.: II, 247
Rolls, Charles: II, 177
   Sarah: II, 177
Rothwell, Anderson: II, 467; III, 32
   Charles: LB, 9, 12
   Claiborn: LB, 20
   Harriet C.: II, 497
   Henry: II, 497
   John: LB, 64; II, 153
   Martha: II, 497
   Sarah Mildred: II, 467
   Theodore: II, 497
   Thomas: II, 467; III, 32
Salmon, Caroline M.: II, 379
   Jane: II, 51
   John: LB, 55
   John D.: LB, 55
   Martha: II, 53
   Thomas: LB, 55; II, 51, 53, 379

Sample, Andrew: II, 453
  Stephen F.: II, 457; III, 38
Sandidge, John: LB, 20
Sandridge, Benjamin: LB, 40
  Fanny: LB, 40
  Jane: LB, 40
  Joshua: LB, 40
  Susannah: LB, 40
Saunders, James W.: II, 353; III, 158, 232
  John S.: III, 222
Schenk [or Schink]
  Cornelius: LB, 10, 15, 34
  Peter: LB, 34
Scipe, Harriet: LB, 58
  Michael: LB, 58
Scott, Charles A.: LB, 19, 22
  Daniel: LB, 19
  Elizabeth R.: II, 563
  James: LB, 31
  Jane E.: II, 211
  Jesse: LB, 19
  John: LB, 19, 39; II, 563; III, 46
  Mary David: III, 46
  Pocahontas B.: III, 46
  Robert: II, 211
Scruggs, Benjamin: II, 131
  George A.: II, 87, 109
  Nancy: II, 131
Seay, Andrew J.: II, 419
  Ann Maria: II, 419
  Clement R.: II, 419
  George L.: II, 419
  Martha: II, 419
  Peter H.: II, 419
  Rebecca: III, 256
  William: III, 256
Shackelford, James: II, 239
  Mary Ann: II, 239
  Zachariah: LB, 40; II, 181
Shaffer, Abram: LB, 53
  Charles: LB, 53
  Elizabeth: LB, 53
  Frederick: LB, 53
  George: LB, 53
  John: LB, 53
  Surberry: LB, 53
Shaver, Charles: LB, 24
  Frederick: LB, 24
  Hannah: LB, 24
Shelton, Samuel: LB, 22, 35, 39
  Weath^n: LB, 25
  William: LB, 7, 27
Shepherd, A. J.: III, 254
  Augustine: LB, 20, 25
  Sarah: LB, 25
Shiflett, Anderson: LB, 38
  Anderson R.: II, 357, 359, 387
  Catharine M.: II, 357

Shiflett, Elizabeth: II, 357
   Frances: II, 357
   Harriet: II, 357
   Henrietta: II, 359
   Horace: II, 357
   Joel: LB, 38, 39
   Joseph: II, 359
   Lewis: LB, 35
   Lilbourn: II, 357
   Sarah: II, 387
   Thomas: II, 357
Shultz, Catharine: II, 437
   Elizabeth: II, 437
   Euster: II, 437
   John: II, 437
   John, Sr.: II, 437
   Martha: II, 437
   Nicholas: II, 437
   William: II, 437
Shumate, Bailey: II, 427, 441
Simms [or Sims]
   Bluford: II, 297
   Isaac: LB, 63; II, 297; III, 178
   James: LB, 9, 11; III, 176, 178
   Julia H.: III, 178
   Richard: LB, 9, 11
   Richard D.: II, 297; III, 176, 178
   Richard D., Jr.: III, 178
   Sarah Ann: II, 297
Simpson, John, Jr.: II, 167
Slaughter, Celeste P. C. L.: II, 229
   Charles R.: II, 229
   Elizabeth A.: II, 229
   George: III, 262
   John: LB, 31
   John F.: II, 229
   Mary: LB, 31
   Mary J.: II, 229
   Mary R.: II, 229
   Robert: II, 229
   Robert B.: II, 229
   Robert L.: LB, 31
   Samuel M.: II, 229
   Sarah F. A. W.: II, 229
   Waddy T.: LB, 31
Smith, Austin: LB, 1
   Charles: II, 547
   Christopher T.: II, 395
   Elizabeth: LB, 43
   Frances Ann: II, 521
   Harriet: LB, 43
   Jacob: II, 395, 521
   Jane A.: II, 547
   Jefferson: LB, 54
   Joel: LB, 43, 54
   Joshua: III, 22
   Mary: LB, 1
   Polly: LB, 68

Smith, Rice: LB, 49
  Robert P.: II, 547
  William: LB, 34, 68; II, 305; III, 7, 22, 60, 70, 74
Smithson, Samuel: LB, 23
Snead [or Sneed]
  Benjamin: II, 357, 359, 387
  Cynthia: LB, 26
  Elijah: LB, 6
  Elizabeth: LB, 26
  Holeman: LB, 26, 31
  John: LB, 6
  Nancy: LB, 31
  Nicholas: II, 449
  Richard: LB, 72
  Robert: II, 449
  Stapleton C.: II, 315, 357, 359, 387; III, 132, 140
  Stapleton Emmett: III, 140
Snow, Mary E.: III, 258
  Reuben D.: III, 258
  Richard: LB, 5
  Sarah C.: III, 258
  Susan A.: III, 258
Soloman, Elizabeth: LB, 9, 13
  John D.: LB, 9, 12
  Mary: LB, 9, 12
  Peggy: LB, 9, 13
  Thomas: LB, 9, 13
Southall, V. W.: LB, 80
  Valentine W.: LB, 79
Sowell, Benjamin: LB, 52
  Elisha: LB, 40
  Lewis: II, 425, 519; III, 244
Speace, Jacob: LB, 60
  Susan: LB, 60
Spencer, Catharine M.: II, 17
  Charles: II, 17, 41
  Elizabeth: II, 41, 343
  Elizabeth W.: II, 23
  Elizabeth Wray: II, 17
  Julia: II, 41
  Malinda F.: II, 409
  Martha M.: II, 41
  Polly: LB, 25
  William: LB, 25, 60; II, 343
Spiece, John B.: II, 13, 63, 71, 73; III, 252
Spiller, Colin C.: II, 491
  George G.: II, 491
Spradling, David: LB, 72
  Virginia: II, 103
Sprouce [or Sprouse]
  George: II, 117
  Randal: II, 59
  Tandy: II, 13
  Tipton: II, 117
Squair[?], Andrew: LB, 54
Stevens, William: LB, 45
Stewardson, William: LB, 74
Stockton, Catharine: III, 86, 278

Stockton, Catharine M.: II, 303
   John N. C.: II, 303; III, 86, 278
   Richard C.: II, 303
   William T.: II, 303
Stout, Isaiah: LB, 61
Strange, Elizabeth: LB, 28
   Hudson: III, 160
Strayer, Jacob: II, 133
Stribling, Erasmus: LB, 56
Suddarth, James W.: II, 465; III, 26
   Thomas: LB, 38
   William: LB, 45, 55; II, 131
   William H.: II, 465
Sutherland, Joseph: LB, 24
Sutton, Jeremiah: III, 124
   Joshua: III, 124
   Wisdom: III, 124
Taylor, Benjamin: LB, 69
   Charles W.: II, 279
   John: II, 25
   Susan: II, 25
   William: LB, 71, 80
Teel, Lewis: II, 391, 403
Terrill [or Terril]
   Charles: LB, 10, 17
   Chiles: LB, 10, 15, 27
   Dabney: LB, 22
   David: II, 311
   George M.: II, 311
   Jackson M.: II, 311
   James H.: LB, 28; II, 527
   John: LB, 4
   Lucy Ann: LB, 22, 37
   Lucy C.: II, 499
   Martha J.: LB, 22
   Martha W.: LB, 75
   Mary Jane: LB, 22
   Reubin: LB, 4; II, 311
   Richard: LB, 22, 37, 51
   Susan: II, 311
   Virginia: LB, 22, 51
   William: LB, 75
Thacker, Benjamin: LB, 20; II, 59, 553
   Betsey: II, 63
   Celia: II, 475
   Elizabeth: II, 317
   Elly: LB, 71
   Ezekial: II, 59, 103
   Francis L.: II, 317
   Henry: II, 59, 103
   Isham: II, 553
   Jerusha: LB, 20
   Jesse: LB, 71
   John: LB, 19
   Julia: II, 317
   Lindsay: II, 475
   Martin: II, 351

Thacker, Mary B.: II, 317
  Mildred: II, 351
  Nathaniel: LB, 60
  Patsy: II, 447
  Samuel: II, 351
  Sarah: II, 553
  Susan: II, 63
  William: II, 351
  Wilson: II, 317
Thomas, Ann: II, 313
  Charles: LB, 77
  Charles L.: LB, 76, 77, 79, 80; II, 111
  Elizabeth: II, 313
  Frances: LB, 79
  Hudson: II, 213
  James: II, 213
  Jesse: II, 159
  John: LB, 80
  John J.: II, 11
  John L.: LB, 76, 77, 79, 80; II, 111, 159
  John W.: LB, 79
  Julia Ann: III, 202
  Mary: II, 313
  Mildred: II, 313
  Nancy: II, 159
  Nicholas: LB, 76
  Obediah: LB, 24
  Ralph: II, 213
  Rebecca: II, 213
  Reuben: II, 213, 313
  Robert W.: LB, 79
  Samuel: III, 202
  William: II, 313
Thomason, Abias: LB, 42
  Catharine: LB, 71
  Rice: LB, 71
  Sarah: LB, 42
Thombs, Margaret: II, 207
  Samuel: II, 207
  William: II, 207
Thomerson, Sarah: II, 263
Thompson, Bernard B.: II, 541
  Catharine B.: II, 185
  David: LB, 1; II, 15, 185
  Dorothy C.: II, 185
  Edmund J.: II, 309, 541
  John: LB, 9, 13
  Nathaniel: LB, 75
  Nathaniel, Jr.: II, 185
  William: LB, 1
Thomson, David: LB, 5
  John: LB, 5
  Robert: LB, 5
Thurmond, Benjamin: LB, 10, 16, 47; II, 83, 199, 397
  Benjamin W.: III, 84
  Elisha: II, 281, 285
  Elisha H.: III, 34, 84
  John: II, 439

Thurmond, Jordan: II, 529
   Mary Ann: II, 429
   Mary D.: III, 84
   Melinda C.: III, 34
   Rebecca: II, 84
   Theodore L.: III, 84
   Thomas L.: III, 84
   Turner: II, 397
   William: II, 83
   William C.: III, 84
   William M.: II, 83, 199
Tilman, Paul, Jr.: III, 248
Timberlake, John: II, 415, 558; III, 46
   Walker: III, 36
Tinden, David: III, 22
   Ephraim: III, 250
Tinder, Mary J.: III, 250
   William C.: III, 250
Tinsley, John: LB, 10, 17
Townley, Ann: LB, 50, 66
   Buckner: LB, 66
   Elizabeth: LB, 50
   Mann: LB, 50, 66
Travillian, Elizabeth: II, 187
   George: II, 187
   James: LB, 49; II, 187, 189
   John: II, 189
   Nelson: LB, 49; II, 189
   Susanna: LB, 47
   Thomas: LB, 10, 16, 47, 49; II, 187
Trice, Anderson: III, 40
   Benjamin F.: II, 191; III, 264, 266
   Catharine: II, 469 [398]
   James A.: II, 469 [398]
   Lucy Ann: III, 266
   Thomas N.: III, 40
   William A.: III, 264
True, Martin: II, 163
Tucker, George: III, 15
   St. George: III, 220
Tuley, William, Jr.: LB, 28
   William, Sr.: LB, 28
Tullock, William: II, 3
Tunstill, Stokes: III, 144
Turner, Charles: LB, 4
   George: LB, 4
   Henry: II, 105
   Judith: LB, 4
   Kesiah: LB, 4
   Mary: LB, 4
   Mary C.: III, 218
   Maryan: LB, 4
   Matthew: LB, 4, 73, 75; II, 125
   Reuben: LB, 4
   Robert: LB, 4
   William: LB, 4
   William D.: III, 218
Tutwiler, Martin: II, 419

Twyman, Joseph W.: II, 503, 509
Tyree, Garrett: II, 45
Ure, ____: II, 45
   Louisa: II, 45
Vermillion, James: III, 122
Via, Daniel: II, 287
   Menoah: LB, 75
   Reuben: II, 393
   Tarlton: II, 393
   Thomas M.: III, 192
   William W.: III, 122
Vowles, John: III, 266
Walker, Eliza: LB, 63
   Francis: LB, 8, 21
   James: LB, 10, 17
   John: LB, 10, 15, 29
   Lawrence: II, 389
   Martha: II, 389
   Patsey: LB, 63
Wallace, Charles: III, 48
   George: III, 48
   James H.: III, 48
   John: LB, 54; III, 48, 60, 74
   John G.: III, 74
   Lavinia: III, 48
   Mary Pilson: III, 60
   Michael: III, 48
Walters, Benejah: LB, 45
   George: LB, 45
   James O.: LB, 76
   James Old: LB, 45
   Joseph: LB, 45
   Margaret: LB, 45
   Mores[?]: LB, 45
   Polly: LB, 45
   William: LB, 45
Walton, Mathew P.: LB, 61
   Morning Hart: LB, 61
Warwick, Andrew S.: II, 381, 559
   Mary E.: II, 381
   Rachel C.: II, 559
Wash, William L.: II, 447, 449
Washington, Ann C.: LB, 10, 17
   Francis M.: LB, 10, 17
Watson, Andlyenly[?]: LB, 46
   Anleonia[?]: LB, 48
   Daniel E.: III, 50
   E. R.: II, 527
   Egbert R.: II, 489
   James: LB, 26, 45, 47
   James A.: II, 507; III, 54
   James B.: LB, 40
   James R.: II, 211, 337, 401
   John: LB, 9, 12, 26, 48, 49, 50; II, 9, 337, 401
   Lucinda: LB, 46, 48
   Lucy: LB, 4
   Martha: LB, 47, 51
   Matthew: LB, 9, 12

Watson, Matthew P.: LB, 57; III, 172
   Mildred: LB, 4, 9, 12
   Opie Norris: III, 172
   Richard P.: LB, 45, 46, 48, 51, 59
   Sarah: LB, 3
   William: LB, 3, 4, 9, 12, 34, 45, 47, 51, 59, 70, 73
Watts, David: III, 124
   Ebenezer: II, 107
   Elijah: LB, 24
   Jacob: LB, 32
   James D.: III, 292
   John B.: II, 19, 255
   Mildred B.: II, 19
   Nancy: II, 19
   Nathan: II, 19
   Phillips: II, 19
   Thomas B.: III, 292
   William B.: II, 19
Wayland, William H.: III, 290
Wayman, Francis: II, 167
   John: II, 167
Weatherhead, William: LB, 36
Wedderfield, James: II, 475
Weidemyer, John F.: II, 77
   John M.: II, 77
Wells, John C.: LB, 75, 76
   Mary: LB, 75
   Thomas: LB, 75
Wertenbaker, Christian: LB, 20
   Edmund: II, 511
   Thomas J.: II, 461
   William: II, 415, 461, 563; III, 46
West, James: LB, 58
   James H.: LB, 52, 58
   Thomas: LB, 52, 58
Wheat, Arthelia E.: III, 260
   Arthur E.: II, 431
   Elijah T.: II, 431; III, 260
   Elizabeth: II, 431
   Franklin: II, 431
   Horatio T.: III, 260
   Letty Ann: II, 431
   Rezen: II, 431
Wheeler, Benjamin: LB, 51, 76; II, 429
   Benjamin J.: II, 455
   Eliza: II, 327
   John: LB, 33; II, 327
   Joshua: II, 327
   Joshua N.: II, 327
   Julia Ann: II, 455
   Mary Ann: II, 327
   Mary E.: II, 455
   Micajah: LB, 51; II, 327, 455
   Robert: LB, 33, 51; II, 553
White, Chapman: LB, 68
   Crenshaw: LB, 40
   Garrett: II, 79, 165
   Henry: LB, 64; II, 35, 39, 99, 101, 125, 127, 161, 463

White, Jeremiah: II, 295
  John: II, 79
  Mildred: LB, 68
  Peter: II, 87, 113, 115, 523
  Samuel G.: II, 463
  William: LB, 35
Wilhoit, Ezekiel: II, 373, 375
  Martha Jane: II, 375
  Sarah Ann: II, 373
Williams, Elisha J.: III, 268
Wilkerson, Anthony P.: LB, 71
  John: II, 407
Wills, Frederick William: LB, 1
  Jane: LB, 73
  Thomas: LB, 73
Wingfield, Alonzo: II, 525
  Charles: LB, 5, 10, 17
  Charles, Jr.: LB, 2, 5, 9, 11
  Charles L.: III, 66
  Chasteau: II, 525
  Christopher: LB, 10, 18, 52
  Edward: LB, 38, 52; II, 481
  Francis: II, 525,
  Henrietta A.: II, 525
  John: LB, 52
  John B.: II, 399
  John J.: II, 525; III, 66
  John M.: II, 351
  Joseph: LB, 10, 17, 80; III, 66
  Joseph F.: LB, 52; III, 26
  Marcellus J.: II, 525
  Mary C.: II, 399
  Mary Rebecca: III, 244
  Mathew: LB, 38; II, 317
  Nancy: LB, 52
  Polly: LB, 38
  Reuben: LB, 52
  Richard: II, 399
  Thomas: III, 66, 244
Winn, John: LB, 79
Winns, Debora: LB, 54
  James: LB, 54
  Jane: LB, 54
  Patsey: LB, 54
  Patterson: LB, 54
  Samuel: LB, 54
Witt, James Lewis: LB, 21
  John: II, 261
  Lewis: LB, 21
Wolfe, Ezra M.: II, 173
  Ezriah M.: II, 291
Wood, Achilles: III, 194
  Alfred C.: II, 331; III, 9
  Anne: LB, 41; II, 240, 241
  Antoinette: II, 240, 241
  Benjamin: III, 42, 168
  Chapman M.: III, 192
  Clifton R.: III, 192

Wood, Cornelia: II, 240, 241
  David: LB, 26, 32; II, 121; III, 234
  Drury: LB, 29, 34, 48; II, 241; III, 76, 126
  Ephraim: LB, 76
  Francis: II, 121, 411
  George W.: III, 13
  Henry: LB, 41; II, 413
  Isaac N.: III, 13
  James: LB, 18; II, 411, 413
  Jerome B.: III, 142
  Jesse: III, 13
  John: LB, 4, 43
  John, Jr.: III, 168
  John H.: II, 23
  John M.: III, 192
  John T.: II, 455; III, 248
  Julianna: III, 234
  Lucinda: II, 413
  Lucy Ann: III, 192
  Martha (Maupin): III, 192
  Mary: II, 240, 241
  Mary Ann J.: II, 329
  Mary Carter: II, 23
  Mary Frances: III, 13
  Mildred L.: II, 329; III, 9
  Polly: LB, 41
  Rebecca: II, 411, 413
  Rice W.: II, 25, 69, 241
  Robert: II, 121
  Robert W.: III, 17
  Rutha: III, 194
  Samuel: LB, 32, 60; III, 194, 230
  Sarah: II, 240
  Sarah Ann Elizabeth: II, 411
  Sarah Jane: III, 13
  Thomas: LB, 66; II, 239, 240, 241, 329, 331; III, 9, 62
  Warner: III, 17
  William: LB, 10, 16, 40; II, 121
  William D.: III, 192, 234
  William H.: II, 411
  William T.: III, 192
Woodall, Charles: LB, 2
Woods, Andrew M.: III, 110, 114
  Andrew N.[?]: III, 188
  George M.: LB, 47, 50, 59, 61, 74, 77; II, 289, 381, 559; III, 112, 114, 188
  George Matthews: LB, 18
  George W.: III, 110
  Jacob Warwick: III, 112
  James: LB, 50; III, 70, 74
  John: III, 50
  Martha J.: III, 110, 188
  Mary E.: III, 114
  Micajah: LB, 28, 37, 44, 69
  Richard: LB, 18
  Sarah E.: III, 98
  Sarah M.: III, 50
  William: LB, 9, 13, 18, 19, 25, 33, 44, 49, 52, 53, 60; II, 99, 255, 381, 391, 547, 559; III, 98, 112, 114

Woods, William, Col.: III, 110, 188
  William A.: III, 110, 114, 188
Woodson, Ann S.: II, 113
  Augustine: LB, 78; II, 347
  Daniel: II, 113
  Edwin: III, 28
  Elizabeth: II, 554
  John: II, 143, 455
  Lindsay: II, 347; III, 276
  Lucy T.: II, 417
  Martha: II, 495
  Mary E.: II, 523
  Mary Elizabeth: II, 115
  Milner: III, 28
  Samuel: LB, 6
  Stephen: II, 93, 113, 115, 523, 554
  Tarlton: LB, 20, 33, 69
  Tarlton, Jr.: II, 85
  Tucker: LB, 6; II, 347
  Warren: II, 93, 113
  Willey Jane: II, 417
  William D.: II, 417
Woody, Samuel: LB, 32
Wren, Henry: II, 315
  John: II, 315
  Mary: II, 315
  William: II, 315
Yancey, Charles: LB, 3, 32, 41, 46, 51, 55
  Jechonias: LB, 3, 32, 55, 58, 77; II, 441; III, 7
  Jeremiah: LB, 3
  Joel: LB, 3, 23, 77
  Margaret: LB, 3
  Martha: LB, 77
  Ralph H.: LB, 55
  Uriah K.: LB, 61
Yates, Boswell P.: II, 309, 481; III, 56, 106, 142
  Thomas C.: II, 481, 485
Young, Andrew H.: II, 5
  David: II, 5, 7
  Elmira: II, 7
  Emeline: II, 7
  John O.: II, 5
  Lucian: II, 7
  Samuel H.: II, 7
  William: II, 173

www.ingramcontent.com/pod-product-compliance
Lightning Source LLC
Chambersburg PA
CBHW020647300426
44112CB00007B/281